ISSUES THAT CONCERN YOU

Nuclear Power

Arthur Gillard, *Book Editor*

GREENHAVEN PRESS
A part of Gale, Cengage Learning

GALE
CENGAGE Learning

Detroit • New York • San Francisco • New Haven, Conn • Waterville, Maine • London

Elizabeth Des Chenes, *Managing Editor*

© 2012 Greenhaven Press, a part of Gale, Cengage Learning

For more information, contact:
Greenhaven Press
27500 Drake Rd.
Farmington Hills, MI 48331-3535
Or you can visit our Internet site at gale.cengage.com

For product information and technology assistance, contact us at

Gale Customer Support, 1-800-877-4253
For permission to use material from this text or product, submit all requests online at
www.cengage.com/permissions

Further permissions questions can be e-mailed to permissionrequest@cengage.com

Articles in Greenhaven Press anthologies are often edited for length to meet page requirements. In addition, original titles of these works are changed to clearly present the main thesis and to explicitly indicate the author's opinion. Every effort is made to ensure that Greenhaven Press accurately reflects the original intent of the authors. Every effort has been made to trace the owners of copyrighted material.

Cover image Terrance Emerson/Shutterstock.com

LIBRARY OF CONGRESS CATALOGING-IN-PUBLICATION DATA

Nuclear power / Arthur Gillard, editor.
    p. cm. -- (Issues that concern you)
  Includes bibliographical references and index.
  ISBN 978-0-7377-5696-8 (hardback)
  1. Nuclear engineering--Juvenile literature. 2. Nuclear energy--Juvenile literature.
I. Gillard, Arthur.
  TK9148.N823 2011
  333.792'4--dc23

                                                                    2011014082

Printed in the United States of America
1 2 3 4 5 6 7 15 14 13 12 11

CONTENTS

"On April 26, 1986, a major accident occurred at Unit 4 of the nuclear power station at Chernobyl, Ukraine, in the former USSR [United Soviet Socialist Republics]. . . . The reactor's fuel elements ruptured and there was a violent explosion. The 1000-tonne sealing cap on the reactor building was blown off. At temperatures of over 2000°C, the fuel rods melted. The graphite covering of the reactor then ignited. The graphite burned for nine days, churning huge quantities of radiation into the environment. The accident released more radiation than the deliberate dropping of a nuclear bomb on Hiroshima, Japan, in August 1945."[1]

What happened at Chernobyl more than a quarter of a century ago represents for many people the ultimate nuclear power nightmare. At the time many believed that the nuclear power industry would never recover—that public opinion had irrevocably turned against the use of nuclear energy once and for all—and yet nuclear reactors have continued to supply about 20 percent of US electricity, as well as a significant fraction of the world's energy, since that time. Indeed, around the world dozens of new nuclear power plants are now under construction, and many more are planned. What has changed?

One significant factor in the survival of the nuclear power industry is that climate change scientists have almost universally declared a planetary emergency linked to the widespread use of fossil fuels and the resulting "greenhouse gases" that, according to many experts, are already causing harmful effects and that potentially threaten outcomes that would far outstrip the damage done by nuclear accidents like the one at Chernobyl. Some scientists, such as James Lovelock, claim that climate change could even cause "planet-wide devastation worse even than unrestricted nuclear war between superpowers. The climate war could kill nearly all of us and leave the few survivors living a Stone Age existence."[2]

Nuclear power advocates claim that nuclear reactors are an essential tool in averting catastrophic climate change, since nuclear power plants produce energy without emitting greenhouse gases. Interestingly, while many environmental organizations continue to fight against nuclear power, some very prominent environmentalists who long opposed nuclear power are now among the loudest advocates calling for a massive increase in nuclear power to wean the human race off of fossil fuels. Bill McKibben, author of *Eaarth: Making a Life on a Tough New Planet* and founder of the popular climate change website 350.org, puts the argument this way: "Nuclear power is a potential safety threat, if something goes wrong. Coal-fired power is guaranteed destruction, filling the atmosphere with planet-heating carbon when it operates the way it's supposed to."[3]

The debate over climate change and what to do about it may have intensified the nuclear power debate but certainly has not resolved it. Indeed, virtually every aspect of nuclear power is hotly contested, with strong opinions being forcefully put forth on every side of the issue. Consider again the example of Chernobyl, the only nuclear accident serious enough to get the top rating (level 7) on the International Nuclear and Radiological Event Scale, "a major release of radioactive material with widespread health and environmental effects requiring implementation of planned and extended countermeasures."[4] How many people have died, or will die, as a result of that accident? A report by the Chernobyl forum published in 2005 says that 56 deaths were directly caused by the accident—47 accident workers plus nine children who died from thyroid cancer. According to the World Health Organization, 4,000 deaths will eventually result from the event.[5] Noted environmental organization Greenpeace sponsored a report in 2006 claiming an estimated 93,000 terminal cancers had already resulted, while the Russian Academy of Medical Sciences the same year declared that 212,000 people had already died prematurely as a result.[6]

Proponents of nuclear power note that following the accident at Chernobyl, many safety procedures and increased levels of international cooperation and inspection were put into place to prevent

A photo shows the damaged Chernobyl nuclear plant soon after the explosion on April 26, 1986. For those living in the area, it was the ultimate nuclear nightmare.

any such accident from happening again. Opponents of nuclear power continue to use it as an example of how badly things can go wrong. They also point to a more recent example: the March 2011 tragedy in northern Japan, in which radiation was released from a nuclear power plant following a devastating earthquake and tsunami. Meanwhile global power consumption continues to rise even as warnings of the dangers associated with the ongoing use of fossil fuels become more urgent every year. Does nuclear power represent a valuable part of the solution to a global crisis, or is nuclear power itself an unacceptable danger to the human race and the environment? Whatever conclusions one may choose to draw from these questions, the debate over nuclear power has certainly reached a critical turning point. What happens over the next few decades may well have momentous consequences, not only for the nuclear power industry, but potentially for all life on earth.

Authors in this anthology propose a variety of perspectives on nuclear power. In addition, the volume contains several appendixes to help the reader understand and explore the topic, including a thorough bibliography and a list of organizations to contact for further information. The appendix titled "What You Should Know About Nuclear Power" offers facts about nuclear power. The appendix "What You Should Do About Nuclear Power" offers advice for young people who are concerned with this issue. With all these features, *Issues That Concern You: Nuclear Power* provides an excellent resource for everyone interested in this issue.

Notes

1. Greenpeace International, "What Happened in Chernobyl?," March 20, 2006. www.greenpeace.org/international/en/cam paigns/nuclear/nomorechernobyls/what-happened-in-chernobyl.
2. James Lovelock, "Climate War Could Kill Nearly All of Us, Leaving Survivors in the Stone Age," *Guardian* (London), June 29, 2009. www.guardian.co.uk/environment/2009/jun/29/ climate-war-lovelock.
3. *Sentient Times*, "Interview with Bill McKibben," blog entry by Meteor Blades, October/November 2006. www.sentienttimes .com/06/oct_nov_06/interview_mckibben.html.
4. S.Y. Chen and Thomas S. Tenforde, "Optimization Approaches to Decision Making on Long-Term Cleanup and Site Restoration Following a Nuclear or Radiological Terrorism Incident," *Homeland Security Affairs*, January 1, 2010. www.hsaj .org/?fullarticle=6.1.4.
5. Rosie Dimanno, "Part 1: Life Returns to an Eerie Chernobyl," TheStar.com, October 17, 2009. www.thestar.com/news/world/ article/711752--dimanno-life-returns-to-an-eerie-chernobyl.
6. John Vidal, "Hell on Earth," *Common Dreams*, April 26, 2006. www.commondreams.org/headlines06/0426-01.htm.

ONE

An Overview of Nuclear Power

AP Online

> AP Online is a part of the Associated Press, an American news service. In the following viewpoint the author explains the basics of producing nuclear power. The article claims that an expansion of nuclear energy will be neither cheap nor easy and will face obstacles, but it is being considered by environmentalists. According to the author, nuclear power uses an energy source to create steam, which then drives a turbine to generate electricity. The nuclear power plant relies on nuclear fission to produce heat. The viewpoint also addresses the safety concerns of nuclear waste.

Thanks to global warming, nuclear energy is hot again. Its promise of abundant, carbon emissions-free power is being pushed by the president and newly considered by environmentalists. But any expansion won't come cheap or easy.

The enormous obstacles facing nuclear power are the same as they were in 1996, when the nation's last new nuclear plant opened near the Watts Bar reservoir in Tennessee after 22 years of construction and $7 billion in costs.

Waste disposal, safe operation and security remain major concerns, but economics may be the biggest deterrent. Huge capital costs combine into an enormous price tag for would-be investors.

There is also fervent anti-nuke opposition waiting to be re-stoked. Jim Riccio of Greenpeace said nuclear advocates are exploiting global warming fears to try to revive an industry that's too risky to fool with.

"You have better ways to boil water," Riccio said.

But environmentalists aren't in lockstep on the issue. Bill Chameides, chief scientist for Environmental Defense, said anything that helps alleviate global warming must be an energy option.

"I think it's somewhat disingenuous that folks who agree that global warming is such a serious issue could sort of dismiss it out of hand," he said. "It's got to be at least considered."

The U.S. has 104 commercial reactors which supply about 20 percent of the country's power. The Department of Energy projects a 45 percent growth in electricity demand by 2030, meaning 35 to 50 new nuclear plants will be needed by then just to maintain nuclear's share of the energy market, said Scott Peterson of the Nuclear Energy Institute, the industry's chief lobbyist.

That growing demand, not global warming, "has been the single biggest factor in companies looking at building large nuclear plants again," Peterson said.

The Nuclear Regulatory Commission has been notified that several companies will pursue licenses for up to 33 new reactors, with the first one online in seven years at the earliest.

Earlier this year, projects at existing plants in Illinois and Mississippi received permits for their proposed sites, but it's no guarantee they'll be the first projects completed.

Many of the new plants are proposed in areas that already have existing plants where there is more acceptance of nuclear energy. President Bush visited one of those spots recently when he promoted nuclear energy at the Browns Ferry's Unit 1 reactor in Alabama.

But any major expansion will require selling nuclear in new places, where local opposition may be intense and winning approval may be costly.

"This isn't just a bunch of environmentalists who think this is a bad idea," Riccio said. "It's most people who aren't being paid to think otherwise."

Nuclear power is produced when neutrons split the nucleus of uranium atoms, releasing heat which is used to boil water and produce the steam that drives a plant's turbines. The process is emissions-free and the radioactive waste is contained inside the plant.

The waste is currently stored at individual plants, awaiting permanent transfer to the national Yucca Mountain Repository in Nevada. But Yucca Mountain has faced stiff opposition and won't open until the early 2020s at the earliest. By then, it will be too small to hold the waste produced nationally.

Recycling used fuel, which contains 90 percent of its original energy after one use, can reduce waste. "Reprocessing" also produces a plutonium that's nearer to weapons grade, raising fears that widespread reprocessing could increase the risks of nuclear proliferation.

A button of U-235 (pictured) is a radioactive isotope of uranium that is used in the production of nuclear energy.

Nuclear energy critics also see the plants themselves as devastating terrorist targets—"predeployed nuclear weapons," as Paul Gunter of the anti-nuclear Nuclear Information and Resource Service calls them.

While opponents fear catastrophe, money may be what kills a nuclear revival. Peterson estimates each new plant will cost about $3 billion, but the industry has a history of construction delays and cost overruns.

The 2005 energy bill passed by Congress provides subsidies for the first six plants, which the industry sees as a one-time "jump start," Peterson said.

Chain Reaction

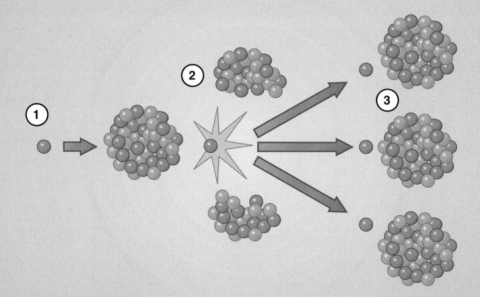

1. A neutron is about to hit the nucleus of a uranium atom

2. The uranium nucleus splits (fissions) into several smaller atoms, releasing heat and several more neutrons.

3. The chain reaction begins: Those neutrons hit other nuclei, causing them to fission, and so on.

Taken from: Gwyneth Cravens, *Power to Save the World: The Truth About Nuclear Energy.* New York: Knopf, 2007, p.51.

"If we can't be competitive after those first few reactors, then companies will stop building them," he said. "No one is building nuclear plants because they have a religious belief in nuclear."

The industry hopes new standardized plant designs will help control costs by taking advantage of cheaper, offsite modular construction. Standardization could also allow plants to share parts and work crews, Peterson said.

He said the new designs are also safer because they incorporate the lessons of Three Mile Island, which had a partial meltdown in 1979 after workers misread a valve and mistakenly thought cooling water was getting into the reactor.

The new systems have fewer valves and less piping, relying primarily on gravity to deliver cooling water to the reactor.

Peterson said the industry has proven it can safely store its waste, and will be able to do so until Yucca Mountain is open. Nuclear plants also have elaborate security, including heavily armed guards trained to deal with various attack scenarios, including multiple truck bombings and suicide attack by wide bodied airplane, similar to the Sept. 11 attacks, Peterson said.

Patrick Moore, a Greenpeace co-founder who's become a fervent nuclear energy advocate and industry consultant, said the industry needs to prepare for such worst case scenarios, but those shouldn't drive the debate over nuclear energy.

Moore said his former environmentalist allies, some of whom now deride him as a corporate shill, are stuck in a Cold War mentality that lumps together the benefits and dangers of nuclear technology.

"You don't ban the beneficial uses of a technology just because that same technology can be used for evil," he said. "Otherwise we would never have harnessed fire."

Chameides of Environmental Defense said he thinks nuclear power is safe and that the waste problem has a technical solution, but he needs convincing to endorse a nuclear resurgence. He's waiting to see the industry move aggressively to address concerns about waste and security. He's also skeptical the nuclear industry can survive without continued subsidies, which he opposes.

"I'm a scientist not an economist," Chameides added. "I'm willing to possibly be wrong."

TWO

There Is Renewed Interest in Nuclear Power

World Nuclear Association

The World Nuclear Association is an international organization that promotes nuclear energy and supports the many companies that comprise the global nuclear industry. In the following viewpoint the authors argue that the nuclear power industry is poised for a surge of growth over the coming decades. According to the authors, factors leading to a likely expansion of the nuclear industry include: increasing demand for energy; concerns over climate change leading to interest in low carbon dioxide–emitting technologies; and increased fossil fuel prices making nuclear energy more competitive. They claim that nuclear plants can be built relatively quickly, particularly if a concerted effort is made, and say that public acceptance for nuclear power has been increasing in recent years.

Since about 2001 there has been much talk about an imminent nuclear revival or "renaissance" which implies that the nuclear industry has been dormant or in decline for some time. Whereas this may generally be the case for the Western world, nuclear capacity has been expanding in Eastern Europe and Asia. Indeed, globally, the share of nuclear in world electricity has remained steady or with slight decline at around 15–16%

since the mid 1980s, with output from nuclear reactors actually increasing to match the growth in global electricity consumption.

Today nuclear energy is back on the policy agendas of many countries, with projections for new build similar to or exceeding those of the early years of nuclear power. This signals a revival in support for nuclear power in the West that was diminished by the accidents at Three Mile Island [in Pennsylvania in 1979] and Chernobyl [in the Soviet Union in 1986] and also by nuclear power plant construction cost overruns in the 1970s and 1980s, coupled with years of cheap natural gas.

Drivers for the Nuclear Renaissance

The first generation of nuclear plants were justified by the need to alleviate urban smog caused by coal-fired power plants. Nuclear was also seen as an economic source of base-load electricity which reduced dependence on overseas imports of fossil fuels. Today's drivers for nuclear build have evolved:

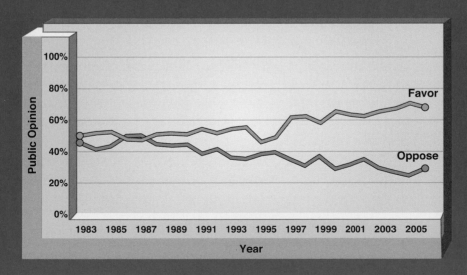

Taken from: Alan M Herbst, *Nuclear Energy Now.* Hoboken: Wiley, 2007, p. 13.

Increasing energy demand. Global population growth in combination with industrial development will lead to a doubling of electricity consumption from 2007 levels by 2030. Besides this incremental growth, there will be a need to replace a lot of old generating stock in the USA and the EU [European Union] over the same period. An increasing shortage of fresh water calls for energy-intensive desalination [removing salt from seawater] plants, electric vehicles will increase overnight (base-load) demand, and in the longer term hydrogen production for transport purposes will need large amounts of electricity and/or high temperature heat.

Climate change. Increased awareness of the dangers and effects of global warming and climate change has led decision makers, media and the public to agree that the use of fossil fuels must be reduced and replaced by low-emission sources of energy. Popular sentiment focuses on renewables, but nuclear power is the only readily-available large-scale alternative to fossil fuels for production of continuous, reliable supply of electricity (ie meeting base-load demand).

Economics. Increasing fossil fuel prices have greatly improved the economics of nuclear power for electricity now. Several studies show that nuclear energy is the most cost-effective of the available base-load technologies. In addition, as carbon emission reductions are encouraged through various forms of government incentives and emission trading schemes, the economic benefits of nuclear power will increase further.

Insurance against future price exposure. A longer-term advantage of uranium over fossil fuels is the low impact that increased fuel prices will have on the final electricity production costs, since a large proportion of those costs is in the capital cost of the plant. This insensitivity to fuel price fluctuations offers a way to stabilize power prices. . . .

Security of supply. A re-emerging topic on many political agendas is security of supply, as countries realize how vulnerable they are to interrupted deliveries of oil and gas. The abundance of naturally occurring uranium and the large energy yield from each tonne of it makes nuclear power attractive from an energy security

Today's proponents of nuclear power argue that the main reasons for increasing its use include increasing energy demands, climate change, economics, the security of the energy supply, and the need for insurance against rising energy costs.

standpoint. A year or two's supply of nuclear fuel is easy to store and relatively inexpensive.

As the nuclear industry is moving away from small national programmes towards global cooperative schemes, serial production of new plants will drive construction costs down and further increase the competitiveness of nuclear energy.

Nuclear Power Capacity Can Be Rapidly Expanded

Most reactors today are built in under five years (first concrete to first power), with four years being state of the art and three years being the aim with modular prefabrication. Several years are required for preliminary approvals before construction.

It is noteworthy that in the 1980s, 218 power reactors started up, an average of one every 17 days. These included 47 in USA, 42 in France and 18 in Japan. The average power was 923.5 MWe [megawatt, or 1 million watts, of electrical energy]. So it is not hard to imagine a similar number being commissioned in a decade after about 2015. But with China and India getting up to speed with nuclear energy and a world energy demand double the 1980 level in 2015, a realistic estimate of what is possible might be the equivalent of one 1000 MWe unit worldwide every 5 days.

A relevant historical benchmark is that from 1941 to 1945, 18 US shipyards built over 2700 Liberty Ships. These were standardised . . . cargo ships of a very basic British design but they became symbolic of US industrial wartime productivity and were vital to the war effort. Average construction time was 42 days in the shipyard, often using prefabricated modules. In 1943, three were being completed every day. They were 135 metres long and could carry 9100 tonnes of cargo, so comparable in scale if not sophistication to nuclear reactors.

Public Acceptance Is Increasing

During the early years of nuclear power, there was a greater tendency amongst the public to respect the decisions of authorities licensing the plants, but this changed for a variety of reasons. No revival of nuclear power is possible without the acceptance of communities living next to facilities and the public at large as well as the politicians they elect.

The Chernobyl disaster marked the nadir [low point] of public support for nuclear power. However, this tragedy underscored the reason for high standards of design and construction required in the West. It could never have been licensed outside the Soviet Union, incompetent plant operators exacerbated the problem, and partly through Cold War isolation, there was no real safety culture. The global cooperation in sharing operating experience and best practices in safety culture as a result of the accident has been of benefit worldwide. The nuclear industry's safety record over the last 25 years is unrivalled and has helped restore public faith in nuclear power. Over this period, operating experience has tripled, from about 4000 reactor-years to more than 14,000 reactor years (plus a similar total in the nuclear navies).

Another factor in public reassurance is the much smaller than anticipated public health effects of the Chernobyl accident. At the time many scientists predicted that tens of thousands would die as a result of the dispersal of radioactive material. In fact, according to the UN's Chernobyl Forum report, as of mid 2005, fewer than 60 deaths had been directly attributed to radiation from the disaster, and further deaths from cancer are uncertain.

One of the criticisms often levelled against nuclear power is the alleged lack of strategy and provision for its long-lived wastes. It is argued that local communities would never be prepared to host a repository for such waste. However, experience has shown in Sweden and Finland that with proper consultation and compensation, mostly in the form of long-term job prospects, communities are quite prepared to host repositories. Indeed in Sweden, two communities were competing to be selected as the site of the final repository.

New Nuclear Power Capacity

With 60 reactors being built around the world today, another 150 or more planned to come online during the next 10 years, and over two hundred further back in the pipeline, the global nuclear industry is clearly going forward strongly. Countries with established programmes are seeking to replace old reactors as well as expand capacity, and an additional 25 countries are either considering or have already decided to make nuclear energy part of their power generation capacity. However, most (over 80%) of the expansion in this century is likely to be in countries already using nuclear power.

A World Nuclear Association exercise "Nuclear Century Outlook" projects possible expansion in world nuclear generating capacity. From a base of 373 GWe [gigawatt, or 1 billion watts, of electrical energy] today it projects at least 1130 GWe by 2060 and up to 3500 GWe by then. The upper projection for 2100 is 11,000 GWe.

THREE

Nuclear Power in the United States Faces Significant Challenges

Philip M. Neches

Philip M. Neches is chairman of Foundation Ventures LLC, an investment bank serving information technology and life science companies. He has a doctoral degree in computer science from the California Institute of Technology. In the following viewpoint Neches argues that because America has not built a nuclear power plant in decades, not many students have been motivated to study nuclear engineering, opting instead for careers in other science and technology fields, such as computer science or biology. The resulting shortage of nuclear engineers poses a significant barrier to building more nuclear power plants in America. According to Neches, numerous other obstacles to revitalizing the American nuclear industry exist, including a complicated regulation system that now makes building nuclear plants an expensive and risky investment. He suggests that the most important step that can be taken to help the nuclear power industry is to promote the education of new nuclear engineers.

Many people think the United States should build more nuclear power plants, after a hiatus of some thirty years. We have significant domestic reserves of uranium. Fission does not generate climate-altering green house gases. Even if we build significant amounts of wind and solar capacity, we will still need more base-load capacity, the kind that operates 24/7/365. I find many of these arguments compelling. However, I remain a pessimist about the ability of new nuclear power plants to make a significant contribution to our energy needs, at least not for a very long time.

Start with the fact that we haven't built a new nuclear plant in over a generation. That means that the profession of nuclear engineering has not been much of a draw for at least that long. Our best and brightest STEM (Science, Technology, Engineering and Mathematics) students went into other fields, like computer science, biology, or even finance. The breakthroughs they achieved over the last generation have transformed the way we live, giving us the Information Age, the biotechnology revolution, and the financial meltdown [of 2007]. Oops, can't win 'em all.

As a consequence, we do not have the cadre of engineers to build and operate lots of new nuclear plants. People with experience are a vanishing breed: at the ends of their careers, retired, or dead. We really have only three choices: import experienced engineers, outsource to foreign engineers, or educate our own engineers.

France Has a Vibrant Nuclear Power Industry

If we import engineers, the best source is France. While the US, and most of the rest of the First World, stopped building nuclear power plants, the French kept at it. Their nukes provide most of their electricity.

They did it by completely centralizing control of the industry. Plants are identical—just like Intel's "copy exactly" strategy. Operators trained at one plant can work at any of hundreds of plants, where their American counterparts would have to start training from scratch at each plant, sometimes at another reactor at the same plant. There are no years of delay due to reviews and lawsuits, because the design is already approved. The French still have to deal with long-lived radioactive waste, but at least they have one place to do it.

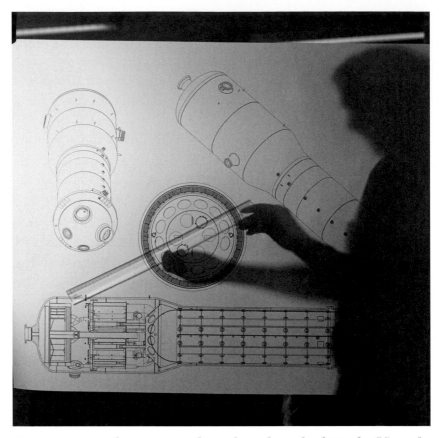

Because no nuclear energy plants have been built in the United States for more than a generation, the supply of engineers trained to build and operate the plants has dwindled.

Central bureaucracy, subsidies, strict regulation, trampling on local prerogatives: to learn from France would be *pâté en croûte de rien* ["pie from scratch"] for the American Right. That's humble pie to us Anglophones.

We could outsource. That would mean China, which has announced ambitious plans to build lots of nuclear power plants. Since China has only a few operational power reactors, they know that they have to build an industry to build the plants. Their institutions of higher education are only too glad to accept the challenge of training a new generation of nuclear engineers. But it will take a while.

In the mean time, China has entered into joint ventures with the few companies with nuclear power technology experience. They make no secret of their intention to use the joint ventures to learn the technology so that they can practice it on their own in short order. Since China already has nuclear weapons and intercontinental missiles, getting adept at commercial power reactor technology does not create a new proliferation threat. But one cannot be so sanguine about the shift in economic leverage.

The final alternative is to educate a new generation of nuclear engineers here at home. We still have the finest research universities in the world. And, thanks to those [expletive deleted] financial engineers, most of them need some new revenue right about now. Make that a lot of new revenue. Right now.

The Private Market Is Reluctant to Invest in Nuclear Power

There are many other obstacles to renewal of the nuclear industry in this country. When we were still building nuclear power plants, it took up to ten years for a plant to get into production. Planning, permitting, public hearings, design, more hearings, re-design, more permits, construction, testing, re-building, and slow ramp up to full power meant that billions of dollars were spent before a single kilowatt-hour was delivered. Finance 101 will tell you that high up-front costs, capped revenue, and high risk do not create an attractive investment.

I saw that up-close and personal as a computer science graduate student in 1977. A group of us visited a development shop at one of the leading power plant construction contractors to see if our new-fangled computer graphics could help. After grasping that the staggering complexity of the plant was way beyond the state of our art in those days, we realized a simpler truth: the economic model of the nuclear power industry simply didn't make sense.

While public sentiment turned against nuclear power in the 1980s, the bond markets [a means, in a free market system, through which money is invested in an organization, with the expectation that there is likely to be a profitable return on the investment] is what really killed the power plant construction industry. The proposed revival of that industry cannot happen without heavy government involvement, because the bond market would still not accept the risk/return ratio without the taxpayer thumb on the scale.

Nuclear Power and Electricity Production in the United States, 2007

Thirty-one states produce electricity using nuclear power plants. Shown here is the percentage of various states' total electricity output generated by nuclear plants in 2007:

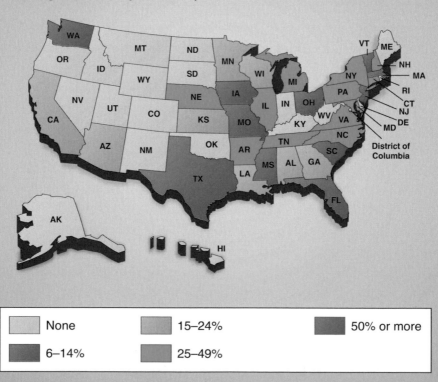

None	15–24%	50% or more
6–14%	25–49%	

Taken from: *DailyME*, "States Making Nuclear Power," 2010. http://dailyme.com/gallery/geography/united-states.html#car45.

Then there is the still unresolved problem of what to do with the nuclear waste. There is much to say on this topic, but I will limit myself to one observation. The amount of time we need to watch over nuclear waste is longer than the longest-lived human civilization—including China.

Maybe France's success can inspire us. But we have a lot of history to overcome, even with bipartisan political support—itself a very endangered species. Anyone who seriously believes that the United States should build more new nuclear power plants should start with revitalizing nuclear engineering at our colleges and universities. The best way to have more nuclear power plants is to go back to school.

FOUR

Irrational Fear Is Limiting Nuclear Power

Ed Hiserodt

> Ed Hiserodt is an expert in power generation technology and an aerospace engineer. In the following viewpoint he argues that nuclear power is not an alternative energy to fear. Hiserodt discusses the ways in which the United States' irrational fears concerning nuclear power are preventing the country from developing new domestic nuclear power plants like other countries are. He also discusses the energy options available and contends that nuclear power is the safest and most logical choice, despite the fear that some have concerning it.

The site of what is arguably the world's leading research program in nuclear energy lies just a short drive from the city of Marseille through the picturesque and romantic countryside of southern France. At Cadarache, the Commissariat a l'energie atomique, the French atomic energy agency, operates a complex of research facilities that is soon to be the home of ITER, the International Thermonuclear Experimental Reactor, which will be the most advanced and powerful Tokamak fusion reactor ever built. This reactor is being funded by the EU, China, Russia, the United States, and others. . . .

In the United States, where nuclear energy technology was invented, only 19.4 percent of electricity is supplied by nuclear power plants. In France, by comparison, 78.5 percent of electricity is generated by nuclear power. The situation is much the same in other European nations. Lithuania, Slovakia, and Belgium all generate more than half of their electricity using nuclear power. Other nations producing more than 40 percent of their electricity using nuclear power include Ukraine, Sweden, Bulgaria, Armenia, and Slovenia. Meanwhile, a growing list of nations, including Russia, China, South Korea, Taiwan, and India, have nuclear power plants under construction.

Notably absent from that list is the United States. Hamstrung by irrational fears, miles of red tape, and onerous bureaucratic regulatory obstacles, no new domestic nuclear power plants have been ordered and built in America for over 30 years, even though the United States has the largest per capita demand for energy. The resulting lack of new nuclear capacity in the face of rising energy demand brings on short-term and long-term consequences. Short-term problems caused by a lack of electrical capacity include rolling blackouts, disruptions in daily life like stopped elevators, non-working traffic signals, loss of refrigerated products, etc. Among long-term problems we face rising electrical costs, termination of marginal industries, and no industrial expansion, among many, many others. Those consequences are entirely unnecessary because nuclear power provides an economical and safe method of producing abundant electricity. . . .

Energy Options

The only really viable alternatives for future large-scale generation lie with the four technologies that already provide the bulk of the nation's power: hydropower, natural gas, nuclear, and coal. Of those, hydropower, providing 6.5 percent of U.S. electricity, has already peaked, and is likely to undergo a slow decline in usage in the future as smaller dams are dismantled to restore the natural course of some rivers. That leaves natural gas, coal, and nuclear power as options.

While natural gas has been highly touted as an energy source because it is considered a relatively clean fuel and because gas plants are relatively inexpensive to build, gas is an unlikely candidate for future large-scale power generation. During the 1990s, construction of gas-fired plants, which now provide 18.7 percent of U.S. electricity, increased because of relatively low fuel prices. In recent years, however, natural gas prices have increased substantially.

Moreover, domestic gas supplies are likely to be insufficient to support long-term expansions in gas-fired generation, even if domestic gas production increases. . . .

Gas isn't going away any time soon, but it is clearly not the best solution to the nation's long term need for energy. Coal, which already provides almost 50 percent of U.S. electricity, is a better option because the United States holds the world's largest reserves of the fuel. But even coal—though it will remain a useful fuel far into the future—fares poorly in comparison to nuclear energy. . . .

The Nuclear Option

Even though coal remains an attractive option, nuclear energy is far superior. For one thing, despite the bad press it gets, nuclear is safer. No one in the United States has died as a result of nuclear-power generation. That can't be said for coal. Historically, more than 100 lives have been lost annually at train crossings owing to coal-hauling unit trains.

Those tragic accidents are examples of the numerous accidents related to fossil-fuel energy generation that claim many lives each year. According to scientist and acclaimed science-fiction author Ben Bova, "If you count up the number of people killed in coal mine disasters or oil well accidents and the wars being fought over oil, nuclear power looks positively benign. Then there are the natural gas and propane explosions that kill hundreds each year and destroy millions of dollars' worth of property."

Finally, and far worse still if we are to believe the Environmental Protection Agency (a practice to be carefully considered), coal-fired plants in the United States annually cause 24,000 early deaths—including 2,800 from lung cancer. According to the

EPA, emissions of fine particle pollution (or soot) resulted in an average loss of 14 years of life for the victims, along with 38,200 non-fatal heart attacks and 534,000 asthma attacks each year. . . .

All things being equal, the economics of energy production also favor nuclear energy over coal. Instead of the 100 or so train cars of coal it takes to run the aver age coal plant each day, nuclear energy uses a comparatively tiny amount of uranium for fuel, making nuclear energy very efficient by comparison. The relatively tiny fuel requirements of nuclear power plants result in operational cost savings, and new technology developed by a private team of scientists in Australia and leased to General Electric promises to reduce costs even more.

Presently, nuclear fuel is commonly enriched by a clumsy process using centrifuge technology, but the Australian team has found a way to enrich uranium much more efficiently using lasers. "The technology, said Michael Goldsworthy, a nuclear scientist and leader of the project, may halve enrichment costs, which he estimated accounted for 30 percent of the price of nuclear fuel," the *Sydney Morning Herald* reported on May 27, 2006.

The power stored in uranium fuel boggles the mind. Suppose you have in your hand a penny-sized piece of the uranium isotope U235. It would seem strangely heavy because its density is more than 2.5 times that of the metal in a modern penny. An enormous amount of energy is pent up in the disc, but it is not hot—either thermally or radioactively. With a half-life of over 700 million years it gives up its radioactivity gradually, and being an "alpha emitter," its radiation is too weak to penetrate your skin. You could wear it as a necklace your entire life without any danger.

Let's further suppose you are Mr. and Mrs. Joe Average living in the Midwest. The average amount of heat energy necessary to heat your house through the snowy days and clear, still, cold Iowa nights from October to March is 80 million BTUs—the BTU being a measure of energy required to raise the temperature of one pound of water by one degree Fahrenheit. Not only would the energy stored in that penny-sized bit of uranium be enough to heat your house for one heating season, it would be enough to heat the average house for more than six years! In fact, a single pickup load of U235 has the equivalent energy of the coal carried in 36,500 large coal cars.

Today, most existing nuclear power plants require uranium fuel that is comprised of about 3 percent U235, with the balance being the more abundant U238 isotope. All told, it takes just six truckloads of uranium to power a typical 1,000-megawatt nuclear reactor for a year. . . .

Split More Atoms

Because nuclear fuel contains such a tremendous amount of energy, incurs relatively little in the way of transportation and fuel costs, and currently is used in reactors built decades ago, electricity generated from that fuel in existing reactors is incredibly cheap. In measurements of economic efficiency that take into account production costs, current U.S. nuclear plants come out on top when compared to coal, natural gas, and petroleum. According to the Nuclear Energy Institute, "In 2005, nuclear power had the lowest production cost of the major sources of electricity, with production cost of 1.72 cents/kWh [per kilowatt hour]. Coal had a cost of 2.21 cents/kWh, natural gas 7.51 cents/kWh, and petroleum 8.09 cents/kWh."

The low cost comes from the fact that the initial costs of construction for most existing reactors have long since been recovered. Moreover, new nuclear-power plants carry an initial price tag that is competitive with the cost of new coal-fired plants. The Associated Press reported on March 21 that Duke Energy Corp. "estimated it would cost $1.53 billion to build a single coal-fired power unit at its Cliffside power plant in western North Carolina." That plant would generate 800 megawatts. By comparison, in 1996 General Electric signed a $1.8 billion contract to build an advanced boiling-water nuclear reactor in Taiwan. Under the terms of that contract, GE even agreed to supply the fuel for the 1,350 megawatt facility. Today, according to the Nuclear Energy Institute, a similar plant of 1,450 megawatts "could be built in the U.S. for $1,445 per kilowatt." That works out to approximately $2.1 billion in construction costs. Figured on a per kilowatt basis,

Duke Energy's proposed coal facility will cost $1,912 per kilowatt to build. In other words, at present a reactor can be built in the United States for less money than it takes to build a coal-fired plant.

And imagine how much less expensive reactor construction would be if more than a decade's worth of regulatory obstacles were removed from the path of future nuclear construction. Construction of the Watt Bar 1 nuclear plant in Tennessee was started in 1973 and the plant went on-line in February 1996. Nearly 23 years. (This plant, incidentally, set the record of 512 days of continuous operation without refueling or any maintenance downtime.) Meanwhile in China, according to World Nuclear News, Westinghouse is building four "AP1000 third-generation nuclear power reactors." From start to finish, construction of those plants is expected to take only four years.

As good as existing designs have been, the new ones are even better. The major U.S. players have new passive reactor designs that take advantage of natural convection and gravity to provide cooling without the necessity of pumps. The Westinghouse AP1000 reactors that are to be built in China are expected to cost only $1,200 per kilowatt installed and have robust safety features. General Electric has developed their ESBWR (the Economic Simplified Boiling Water Reactor) with similar safety features and economic advantages. European, Asian, and South African developers have offerings that may advance their technologies over those of the United States.

One of the more noteworthy is Toshiba's 4S (Super Safe, Small and Simple) reactor that is buried in the ground, requires no operator, and provides 10 megawatts of electricity for 30 years without refueling. After 15 years, the neutron reflectors will have to be rotated; otherwise no maintenance is necessary. Toshiba has offered a 4S reactor to the town of Galena, Alaska, at no charge except for the fuel, which would cost less than one-third what the town now pays for diesel fuel. It's a great deal that, like most nuclear plants, is hamstrung by the cost of paperwork. The next step for this village of 675 souls is to come up with $20,000,000 to pay for an environmental impact statement.

The future is bright for nuclear power. The big question is: will the future be bright for an America that abandons nuclear power? Low-cost energy is essential for the future of all Americans. Climbing energy costs weaken the competitiveness of American industry on the world market. Traditionally, Americans have enjoyed cheap, plentiful power, and that has helped give American industry a competitive edge and led to higher standards of living. Nuclear energy, an American invention, can help keep it that way for decades to come.

It is not too late for U.S. utilities to switch from coal and gas to nuclear power. They did it in France, according to PBS Frontline [a Public Broadcasting Service TV series], when the thought of dependence on foreign fuel sources proved intolerable. "A popular French riposte to the question of why they have so much nuclear energy is 'no oil, no gas, no coal, no choice,'" Frontline reported. And it worked. According to Frontline, "Today, nuclear energy is an everyday thing in France." In matters of nuclear power at least, it's about time for America to follow the French example.

FIVE

In the Wake of Japan's Disaster, the United States Must Reexamine Its Policy on Nuclear Power

Henry Sokolski

Henry Sokolski is the executive director of the Non-proliferation Policy Education Center and the editor of *Nuclear Power's Global Expansion: Weighing Its Costs and Risks.* In the following viewpoint Sokolski surveys the world's reaction to the failures at Japan's Fukushima nuclear power plant in the wake of the 2011 earthquake and tsunami. He notes that while many countries are reexamining policies and shutting down older reactors, at least temporarily, President Barack Obama's administration is standing firm in its nuclear policy. Sokolski urges the administration and congress to do a thorough review of US nuclear facilities and safety policies.

Suddenly, watching Japan's desperate water-cannon attempts to stave off successive nuclear meltdowns at the Fukushima Daiichi nuclear-power plant [in March 2011], we are all supposed to be tech-savvy atomic engineers. Out of nowhere, our job as John Q. Public now involves sorting through a blizzard of contradictory headlines

Henry Sokolski, "Policy in Ashes," *Newsweek*, March 20, 2011. Reproduced by permission.

about what is—and just as much, what is not—happening inside a hugely complex nuclear-power plant halfway around the world.

At once, news reports and public officials told us the reactor smoke, fire, and explosions were in no way comparable to the 1986 nuclear disaster at Chernobyl, the worst in history. Yet, in seeming contradiction, we also have been told that these same flare-ups may well end up salting large swaths of Japan with long-lasting radiation producing—as experts put it—potential "Chernobyl-like" results.

If you have been listening at all—and really, it's been nearly impossible not to—the nuclear world we had before Fukushima is radically different from the one we have now. Clearly the disaster response has not gone well. The many experts who initially insisted that Japan's nuclear-safety systems were working because the reactors' containment vessels had not yet been breached now have gone silent. Why? A week into the crisis, two reactors' containment vessels sprang serious leaks. There is more than a chance that radioactivity might also spew from one or more improperly cooled spent-fuel-reactor ponds. That's bad news.

So bad that the focus has turned to casualties. The safety systems, at least as *Newsweek* went to press, had kept the worst of the radiation from spreading far. Some have seized the fact, and the news that no one has yet died, to argue that nuclear power is safe. Stay tuned.

Most world leaders didn't wait to act. Germany announced it would shut down (temporarily, at least) seven of its oldest reactors. Major safety reviews and licensing breathers have also been announced by France, the European Union, Thailand, Switzerland, the Philippines, India, and even China.

The collective pause is striking given that countries like India and China serve as the poster children for the nuclear industry's much-heralded global renaissance. According to the International Atomic Energy Agency, of the 65 reactors currently under construction around the world, just about half of them (32, to be exact) are found in these rapidly emerging countries.

In the U.S., however, President [Barack] Obama and Secretary of Energy Steven Chu repeatedly tried to reassure the American

On March 22, 2011, German chancellor Angela Merkel and Environment Minister Norbert Roettgen announce plans for tougher safety rules for Germany's nuclear power plants. France, the European Union, Thailand, Switzerland, the Philippines, India, and China are also addressing safety issues.

public. But at best they have been playing catch-up to the rest of the world.

When asked early on if the U.S. should put on the brakes, both the president and Chu insisted no. Instead, they proceeded to promote U.S. nuclear power as if the catastrophe at Fukushima hadn't even happened. Regarding the president's imminent trip to Latin America, the White House announced that it would sign a memorandum of understanding on nuclear-power cooperation with earthquake-prone Chile. Meanwhile, the administration is still pushing Congress to approve $36 billion more in federal loan guarantees for the construction of new reactors. Obama and his nuclear team finally did announce a formal safety review on March 17 [2011], but that came a full week after congressional pleas from both pro- and anti-nuke lawmakers making noise on Capitol Hill.

They were adamant and far more sensitive to something the president and his nuclear advisers seemed reluctant to discuss: the fretful fact that nearly a third of the reactors operating in the U.S. are of a similar design as those that have gone so wrong in Japan. More than 20 are nearly identical and are roughly as old. Some are located near earthquake faults; others are on the coast. Where the Japanese are retiring their machines after 40 years of service, though, the U.S. government has decided to extend operating licenses to allow some of these reactors to run for 60 years.

So what, exactly, is going to happen? In announcing the review, Obama said that American nuclear-power plants "have been declared safe for any number of extreme contingencies," which leads one to ask, if you think the hard work has already been done, what's really going to change? Assuming, then, that any real change is going to come from Congress, what questions should be asked?

First, if the U.S.'s Nuclear Regulatory Commission has been extending operating licenses on reactors similar to those in Japan for an additional 20 years, what should the U.S. government and the reactor operators be doing differently to assure they run safely over their projected 60-year lifetime?

Second, the Japanese assumed that the multiple emergency safety-backup systems would all work independently of one another. Instead, they were swamped with water and failed in block. What other fallacious assumptions are underlying nuclear safety?

Tokyo's bungled response has sparked the question of which U.S. agency should be responsible for dealing with a nuclear incident? Currently, it's the Department of Homeland Security. But after Hurricane Katrina, that should be a cause for pause.

Finally, Congress has plans to revise the export control and nonproliferation provisions of the U.S. Atomic Energy Act. They are sure to ask how much sense it makes for the U.S. to offer nuclear cooperation to states that have little or no reactor-operating experience and lack liability insurance that can protect U.S. vendors in the case of an accident. Also, after Iran's peaceful nuclear program (which was based originally on U.S. nuclear cooperation), shouldn't the U.S. be insisting on the toughest non-proliferation conditions not just of prospective customers, but of other nuclear suppliers?

In the wake of Japan's disaster, much of the world has paused to make sure their nuclear house is in order. If Obama and his nuclear team can't see the need to get answers before pushing more nuclear subsidies domestically and orchestrating more deals abroad, we can only hope that the U.S. Congress, with a closer ear to a public that now is trying to make sense of the news from Japan, will.

SIX

Japan's Disaster Should Not Be Used to Thwart Nuclear Power

Matthew Shaffer

Matthew Shaffer is a William F. Buckley Fellow at the National Review Institute. In the following viewpoint Shaffer asserts that the media's disproportionate coverage of nuclear incidents, such as the one occurring at Japan's Fukushima power plant and the Three Mile Island disaster, create a climate of fear around nuclear power. In reality, he contends, all sources of power have some level of risk involved and nuclear power is no riskier than any other major energy source. Shaffer maintains that Japan's nuclear incident should not hold back US nuclear policy.

"Nobody at Three Mile Island was actually hurt or killed, or anything of that nature," remembers John McGaha, formerly a senior executive of Entergy, a Mississippi company that runs and operates nuclear utilities. "Versus if you look at some of the oil and chemical explosions we've had over the years. . . ."

McGaha and other experts tell NRO [*National Review Online*] that Americans are unduly afraid of nuclear energy—in part because of the media's disproportionate, distorted reporting on rare nuclear accidents like Three Mile Island and the recent problems in Japan. McGaha says the most deadly consequence of Three Mile Island might have been how it delayed the advancement of nuclear technology in the U.S.

Yes, officially, one or two incidents of cancer have been attributed to Three Mile Island. But even with those, there's no way to know for sure. All of us have "a 16 percent lifetime chance of contracting cancer," says Robert Henkin, professor emeritus of radiology at Loyola University in Chicago. So, he asks, "If that goes to 16.1 percent, how do you ever pick that out?" We can't be certain there was any harm at all.

And yet the panic at the time outdid the current panic over the Fukushima reactors. "Governor Thornburg was debating whether he would evacuate 20 miles out," Prof. Michael Corradini, chairman of engineering physics at the University of Wisconsin, remembers. And the newspaper headlines during the Three Mile Island crisis suggested much worse. "Strangely enough," Professor Henkin says, Three Mile Island "was actually one of the great successes of the industry."

It's not remembered that way, of course. One reason seems to be that the terminology related to nuclear power has taken on sinister connotations. Consider *radiation*. Think of the panic that the headline "Radiation levels increase by 100 percent" could induce. But in reality, such radiation would be medically beneficial; it would promote "radiation hormesis"—the exercise of the immune system. "We get one unit of radiation per day. When we double that—they've done tests with animals—they show better health. It's like doing pushups," says Gilbert Brown, a professor of nuclear engineering at the University of Massachusetts–Lowell. That doesn't prove we shouldn't worry about *much* higher levels of radiation—but it indicates how our emotional response does not correspond to reality.

And how high are radiation levels in Japan right now? The International Atomic Energy Agency on Sunday said that radiation levels of 5.7 microsivierts per hour were detected at a 35-mile radius from Fukushima. This, Steve Kerekes of the Nuclear Energy Institute says, is "under what a nuclear-plant worker could be exposed to every day for his job" under the Nuclear Regulatory Commission's guidelines. And even that measure may overrate the risk. "They intentionally set the limits very, very low—at much smaller levels than are actually dangerous, to encourage people

Use of Nuclear Reactors, by Country

Nuclear reactors yield only 6 percent of global energy and despite the Japan's March 2011 nuclear explosion, the use of reactors will still increase. The pie charts do not total 100; each simply shows the proportion of use by each country.

Nuclear Reactors In Use
As a percentage of world total:

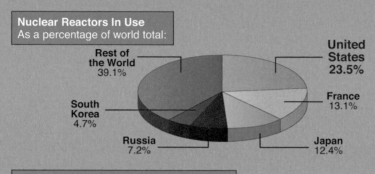

- Rest of the World 39.1%
- United States 23.5%
- France 13.1%
- South Korea 4.7%
- Russia 7.2%
- Japan 12.4%

Proposed Nuclear Reactors
Number of planned nuclear-power stations:

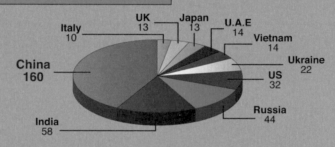

- Italy 10
- UK 13
- Japan 13
- U.A.E 14
- Vietnam 14
- Ukraine 22
- China 160
- US 32
- Russia 44
- India 58

Nuclear-Power Consumption
As a percentage of world total:

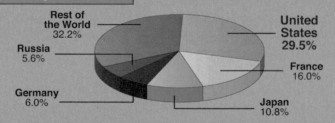

- Rest of the World 32.2%
- United States 29.5%
- Russia 5.6%
- France 16.0%
- Germany 6.0%
- Japan 10.8%

Reliance on Nuclear Power
Percentage of energy produced by nuclear reactors:

Lithuania 76.2 %	Switzerland 39.5%
France 75.2 %	Bulgaria 35.9%
Slovakia 53.5%	South Korea 34.8%
Belgium 51.7%	Sweden 34.7%
Ukraine 48.6%	Japan 28.9%
Slovenia 39.5%	United States 20.2%

Taken from: *Newsweek Online*, "Our Nuclear World," March 20, 2011. www.newsweek.com/2011/03/20/our-nuclear-world.html. Source: World Nuclear Association, BP; Graphic by Stanford Kay Studio; Source: Ranking America http://rankingamerica.wordpress.com.

to be very safe with radiation," Professor Henkin says. Comparing Japan's current levels with the data derived from the decades-long Atomic Bomb Project, which followed people exposed at various distances to the Hiroshima and Nagasaki explosions, Henkin concludes the following: "The dosage that people had to attain to achieve above-average incidence of cancer in a population is orders of magnitude above anything basically anybody [outside of the plants] in Japan is experiencing right now."

Here's another example: *meltdown*. The nuclear experts like to call it "the M-word." "We use the term 'meltdown,' and it conjures up this disaster," Brown says. But a meltdown is not always a catastrophe. "When you say 'car accident,' people know it could be a fender-bender, or it could be fatal. Nobody just assumes it was fatal. It should be the same with a meltdown. There are many scenarios in which a meltdown happens and nobody gets hurt," Brown says.

Here's what a typical meltdown really is, and how it may have happened in Fukushima. At the first sign of danger (to which nuclear reactors are very sensitive—the Fukushima reactors knew about and responded to the earthquake before people felt it), a nuclear reactor automatically shuts down the uranium-fission process by which it produces the vast majority of its heat. But that doesn't stop all energy production. Uranium fission results in several radioactive byproducts, which produce roughly 6 percent of the heat of the normal, functioning reactor—and continue to do so after the fission itself stops. So at this point, nuclear engineers can avoid a meltdown by bleeding away 6 percent of the heat that a normal reactor gives off.

So why didn't this work at Fukushima? It's simple: Diesel generators—the power source for the reactors' cooling systems—got wet. Amazingly enough, the reactors survived the Richter scale 9 earthquake when almost everything in the surrounding area was destroyed. But the tsunami, which came afterward, knocked out the generators. If the diesel generators had been properly equipped to deal with the wave, the Fukushima reactors would be fine. For now, keeping the reactors cool will be a pain, but a devastating meltdown doesn't seem likely.

If the reactor is not sufficiently cooled, two things could go wrong. First, the metal in the containment vessel of the reactor might get so hot that it oxidizes any water that comes near it, producing a hydrogen bubble that could explode, as happened in two Fukushima reactors. The other hazard is that the reactor gets so hot that it partially melts (that is, a *meltdown* occurs, as it has in Fukushima), and if the melting is substantial, that might allow radioactive gases to escape and get mixed in with steam that's on its way out of the plant. Even then, there are more lines of defense: charcoal filters that capture the radioactive particles while allowing the steam and noble gases through, and a double containment system that puts another wall (outside of the reactor) between the fuel and the public. If those don't work, the radioactivity in the surrounding area will rise in proportion to the amount of radioactive byproducts released.

Professor [Bill Miller, of the Department of Nuclear Science and Engineering at the University of Missouri] tells NRO that "the public has the notion that we'll see this molten blob of material escaping into the environment. And that doesn't happen."

Here's a final example: *nuclear contamination*. It's a scary phrase, but what does it mean? Formally, Professor Henkin tells NRO, when a person is contaminated, "that means that person really ought to take a shower." And this, Henkin says, is the highest level of exposure civilians have received from Fukushima.

Even so, many things went wrong in Japan last week [March 2011]. But they're very unlikely to happen in the United States. As Prof. Dennis Beller, a nuclear-engineering researcher at UNLV, tells NRO, "U.S. nuclear plants are generally designed to a higher safety level than those in Japan." To start with, we have more redundant and safer energy sources for our coolers. Also, we now have the technological capability to build reactors with automatic-convection cooling systems. That means no external power source will be required, so meltdowns would be prevented even when all power is shut off.

That's the science. But the more important question going forward is one of policy. All the nuclear-energy experts emphasize that good policy means thinking about tradeoffs—choosing among feasible alternatives, rather than striving for perfection. So consider our options, and the consequences of several alternatives.

First, shutting down the production of new nuclear facilities would mean more reliance on old nuclear facilities, which are less safe. Second, shutting down or phasing out all nuclear facilities would necessitate greater reliance on other energy technologies that have their own dangers. As Professor Brown says, in a refrain common to all the nuclear experts, "Think of the BP [British Petroleum] explosion. Or *Exxon Valdez*. Those were pretty hellacious. And every month there's a coal-mine disaster, and you read about pipelines exploding." He recommends acknowledging that we are in "a pragmatic space. That doesn't mean you don't think every life is valuable. But you're balancing risks, and acknowledging their reality in the real world we live in."

President Barack Obama speaks to the press in March 2011 about Japan's earthquake and tsunami and the subsequent nuclear disaster. He said we need to learn from any mistakes, but he has no plans to change US nuclear policy.

The total death toll from Three Mile Island may have been zero, and Chernobyl claimed, by the estimates of the International Atomic Energy Agency, just 50 lives, despite what nuclear experts describe as the Soviet Union's extreme incompetence. Each lost life is a tragedy. But in the 20th century, hydroelectric dams' bursting, coal-mining disasters, and oil explosions have killed tens of thousands. And that includes just direct deaths from accidents, not indirect deaths from displacement, health problems caused by particulate matter, etc. Statistically speaking, nuclear experts claim, uranium fission is the safest major energy source in the world.

It's possible that media overreaction and misunderstanding of the Fukushima incident will hold back the advance of nuclear energy. Chancellor Angela Merkel has ordered a complete shutdown of Germany's seven oldest nuclear plants. Even if those plants did need to be updated, "You can make additions and updates without shutting down the plants," Professor Beller says. Merkel's restriction of the energy supply, he points out, will exacerbate an energy crisis and hurt "low-income people in particular in Germany."

John McGaha fears the worst for the United States. "Every time there's an event of any kind, even if, when it's all said and done, nobody was hurt—anything that can be symbolic of the risk of nuclear energy provides fodder for the anti-nuclear groups to get on their horse and campaign against the industry." And that will have international repercussions: "We're still seen as the go-to country for any other country that wants to build its own program. The United States' policies and designs set the standard for the rest of the world."

There's some reason for optimism, however. As . . . [Professor] Bill Miller says, "I noticed that the president and Secretary Chu have already stated that it's tragic and we need to learn from it, but that doesn't change the U.S. position on the need for nuclear power."

SEVEN

Nuclear Power Can Help Solve the Climate Crisis

Al Simmons and Doug L. Hoffman

Al Simmons wrote the computer systems software for the world's first weather satellites and spent twelve years working with National Aeronautics and Space Administration scientists developing computer systems involved with predictor models for the earth's atmosphere and for ocean cooling and warming studies. Doug L. Hoffman has worked professionally as a mathematician, a computer programmer, an engineer, a computer salesman, a scientist, and a college professor. In the following viewpoint Simmons and Hoffman argue that nuclear power is the only technology that can supply enough power to meet the world's energy needs in the future without damaging the climate. They claim that some leading US environmental organizations are now in favor of nuclear energy, while others remain opposed on irrational grounds. The authors point out that renewable energy sources such as as wind and solar only operate some of the time (when it is windy or sunny), whereas nuclear power is always available.

Of all the ludicrous, wrong headed and down right stupid things to come out of the Copenhagen Climate Conference [in 2009] perhaps the most annoying was the formation of an ad hoc anti-nuclear umbrella organization. Over a dozen NGOs [nongovernmental organizations] participating in the international "Don't Nuke the Climate" campaign presented government delegates with a giant postcard and 50,000 signatures calling for a nuclear free climate agreement. There are ~6.5 billion people on Earth so the collected signatures amount to 0.000769 percent of the global population. Where do the rest of us sign up for a dingbat free planet?

Speaking on behalf of the "Don't Nuke the Climate Campaign" Charlotte Mijeon of Sortir du Nucleaire France said, "We are here to present the signatures we have collected in the last couple of months for a nuclear free climate agreement. In a very short period of time, 350 organisations from 40 countries collected 50,000 signatures from more than 100 countries on every continent. This shows that thousands upon thousands of people around the globe want a fair climate deal where expensive, dirty and dangerous nuclear energy is not part of the package." . . .

In fact, some of the leading U.S. environmental organizations such as the Environmental Defense Fund have quietly or implicitly adopted a pro-nuclear position. Several years ago Environmental Defense's chief executive played a key role in brokering a deal that killed a Texas plan to vastly expand coal generation, and when the dust settled, it came to be understood that instead there would be much greater reliance on nuclear. But many organizations that have been steadfastly opposed to nuclear—Greenpeace, Friends of the Earth, Union of Concerned Scientists, and Physicians for Social Responsibility—remain firmly opposed.

The anti-nuke crowd claims that it takes 10 years to build a nuclear power plant, yet Westinghouse is doing it in 36 months in China. They claim that nuclear energy's output is trivial because it only supplies 2.4% of total world energy, but that is actually 15% of the world's electricity: 19% in the US, 27% in Finland, 30% in Japan, and 78% in France, some of which is exported to Denmark when the wind doesn't blow hard enough to keep their lights on.

They cite the International Commission on Radiological Protection as saying that any irradiation dose may cause cancers and hereditary disorders. So to be safe, CAT scans [a type of

Although many oppose the use of nuclear power, the pollution caused by other sources of energy, such as this coal-fired power plant, would be significantly reduced by using nuclear power.

computerized X-ray scan], medical X-rays or high flying airplane flights will have to go as well. They claim that nuclear power is too expensive, yet much of the expense is caused by construction delays and the interminable, frivolous law suits brought by the green lobby. . . .

Only Nuclear Power Can Significantly Reduce Greenhouse Gases

The anti-nuke clique claims that nuclear power is a distraction from real climate change solutions. If you are a global warming groupie who ardently believes that sharp cuts in greenhouse gas emissions are urgently required, the only way to accomplish that is nuclear. There is simply no way to build enough wind and solar to provide solid base load electricity to fulfill today's demand let alone the future's. Both the EIA [Energy Information Administration] (US) and the IEA [International Energy Agency] (UN) project world power use increasing significantly in the future, mostly in developing nations. The EIA estimate is 44% from 2006 to 2030. Total energy demand in the non-OECD [Organisation for Economic Co-operation and Development] countries increases by 73%, compared with an increase of 15% in the OECD countries. IEA forecasts 40% energy demand growth by 2030, mostly from fossil fuels.

World electricity generation will increase by 77% from 2006 to 2030, and that is not just from rich, developed nations. Non-OECD countries are projected to account for 58% of world electricity use in 2030. The highly optimistic IEA recommends a shift to low-carbon energy sources for 60% of total electricity production by 2030—renewables maxed out at 37% (including hydro and geothermal), nuclear rising a bit to 18% and plants fitted with carbon capture and storage (ie. coal plants) a paltry 5%. The rest will continue to come from gas, oil and primarily, dirty coal. It will take more than solar/wind power, wishful thinking and snappy yellow vests to satisfy growing world energy demand.

Even if enough renewable generating capacity could be installed in 10 years—the magic deadline to limit projected temperature rise to 2°C—wind and solar are intermittent sources of power, and there is no practical way to store renewable energy until it can be used. Beyond that, the power grid, even in developed nations, is unable to deal with the rapid long distance reshuffling of supply and demand such renewable sources require for efficient use. Best estimates for manageable non-hydro, renewable power tops out at around 35% of total capacity, leaving unanswered the question "where do we get the other 65%?"

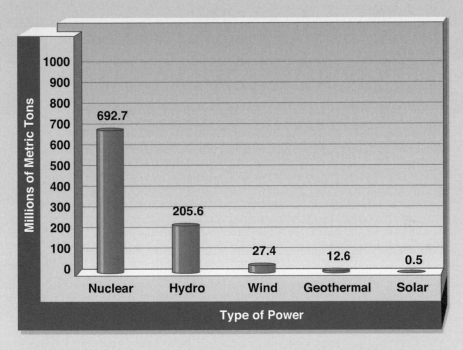

US Electric Power Industry: Net CO$_2$ Emissions Avoided, in Millions of Metric Tons

Millions of Metric Tons

1000	
900	
800	
700	692.7
600	
500	
400	
300	205.6
200	
100	27.4 12.6 0.5
0	

Nuclear   Hydro   Wind   Geothermal   Solar

Type of Power

Taken from: Jonny Abendano, Wednesday Fact Series: "Greenhouse Emissions," *Clean Energy Insight,* September 16, 2009. www.cleanenergyinsight.org/interesting/wednesday-fact-series-greenhouse-emissions.

Unfortunately, even if all the opposition were to evaporate, all the regulatory roadblocks were removed, and costs came down, representatives of the US industry admit that they now are in a position to initiate no more than two or three reactor construction projects per year. At that rate, they could barely replace aging reactors as they are decommissioned. If a dent is to be made in fossil fuel use this just isn't good enough. . . .

The only way to solve this problem is by making nuclear power a national priority in every country. Priority must be given to cutting through the bureaucratic red tape and, above all, providing secure government backed financing for plant construction. Of course that is exactly the opposite of what the neo-Luddite [opposed to modern technology] anti-nuke lobby wants.

EIGHT

Nuclear Power Cannot Solve the Climate Crisis

Jim Rice

> Jim Rice is the editor of *Sojourners* magazine. He was an organizer of the Center for Peace Studies at Georgetown University and has served on the founding national committee and executive committee of the Nuclear Weapons Freeze Campaign. In the following viewpoint Rice argues that nuclear power is not a viable alternative to the toxic and environmentally destructive generation of electricity from coal-fired power plants. According to Rice, the extremely negative health and environmental effects of the uranium industry, as well as the possible consequences of accidents and nuclear terrorism, make nuclear power an unacceptable alternative. In addition, he says, the high cost of investing in nuclear power would prevent the needed investment in energy efficiency and renewable energy, which he sees as the truly environmentally friendly solution to the climate change crisis.

Is nuclear power the "alternative" energy of the future, the way out of our destructive reliance on fossil fuels?

Some environmentalists think so. Patrick Moore, one of the founders of Greenpeace in the early 1970s, argues that "Every responsible environmentalist should support a move" away from coal-generated electricity and toward nuclear plants. "This would go a long way," Moore maintains, "toward cleaning the air and reducing greenhouse gas emissions." That's a bit different than Moore's assessment in a 1976 Greenpeace report, in which he called nuclear power plants—next to nuclear warheads—"the most dangerous devices that man [sic] has ever created. Their construction and proliferation is the most irresponsible, in fact the most criminal, act ever to have taken place on this planet."

What has changed? Is it the technology, or is it Moore? Some of his former associates think it's the latter. Paul Watson, another co-founder of Greenpeace, charged Moore with being a "corporate whore . . . an eco-Judas . . . who has grown rich from sacrificing environmentalist principles for plain old money." Moore is currently paid by the nuclear industry to serve as co-chair of the "Clean and Safe Energy Coalition," an industry front that promotes increased use of nuclear energy, according to *The Washington Post*. . . .

But apart from Moore's dubious impartiality, what about his basic argument? His main case revolves around this fact: "More than 600 coal-fired electric plants in the United States produce 36 percent of U.S. emissions—or nearly 10 percent of global emissions—of CO_2, the primary greenhouse gas responsible for climate change," he wrote in the *Post* earlier this year. "Nuclear energy is the only large-scale, cost-effective energy source that can reduce these emissions while continuing to satisfy a growing demand for power. And these days it can do so safely."

Let's take Moore's arguments one at a time. First, there's no question that coal-fired plants are a problem. Even with state-of-the-art technology using low-sulfur coal, such plants are the single largest source of acid rain and one of the leading contributors to smog. In addition, coal-fired plants emit millions of tons of carbon dioxide, the most significant greenhouse gas, along with mercury, arsenic, beryllium, chromium, and nickel, and heavy metals and chlorine in cooling water discharges—all in all, very bad news. Plus, each plant uses up to a billion gallons of water each day for cooling.

So Moore and his ilk are correct in their indictment of coal's role in our energy future. And it is true that nuclear plants aren't major emitters of greenhouse gases (at least from the plants themselves), so if that were the only issue in power production, nuclear beats coal, hands down. But is nuclear power really the "cost-effective"—and safe—alternative for our energy needs?

Serious Concerns About Nuclear Power

Here are several major areas of concern about nuclear power:

Cost. In its first four decades, nuclear power cost this country more than $492 billion, by conservative estimate—nearly twice the cost of the Vietnam War and the Apollo moon missions combined—according to a study titled "The Economic Failure of Nuclear Power." . . .

Accidents. All 103 nuclear power reactors in the United States, and most around the world, are light water reactors—the same type as Pennsylvania's Three Mile Island [TMI] Unit 2, site of the worst commercial nuclear mishap in U.S. history in 1979. (Recent epidemiological studies found that, in the direct path of the TMI plumes, "lung cancer incidence went up by 300 to 400 percent, and leukemia rates were up by 600 to 700 percent." . . .)

Terrorist attack. The vulnerability of nuclear power plants as potential targets of terrorist attack was recognized long before 9/11 [2001], and concerns have only heightened since then. After Sept. 11, Dr. Edwin Lyman, a physicist and scientific director for the Washington-based Nuclear Control Institute, said that a similar strike on a nuclear plant by a commercial airliner "would in fact have a high likelihood of penetrating a containment building" and that as a result "the possibility of an unmitigated loss of coolant accident and significant release of radiation into the environment is a very real one." In other words, nuclear power plants contain the potential to turn a conventional terrorist attack into, in effect, a massive "dirty bomb," with the resultant spread of radioactive material. . . .

Other health and safety issues. No reactor in the world is, of course, completely safe. Design-based threats will never be completely eliminated, and human error is always a possibility in any endeavor. Along with the most cataclysmic accidents involving the reactor core, other potential large-scale mishaps include a failure of the cooling system required for the highly radioactive spent fuel stored on reactor sites, which could lead to a massive release of radiation. Even apart from major, catastrophic accidents, smaller radiation exposures are a fact of life for those working in or living near nuclear plants.

Uranium Mining Is Highly Toxic

But it's possible that the reactor site itself is the least-dangerous part of the nuclear fuel cycle. The peril begins with the mining of uranium. Jim Harding, an energy and environment consultant, said, "We easily forget the awful legacy on the front end of the fuel cycle—uranium mill tailings contain 85 percent of the radioactivity of the original ore body . . . quite dangerous, and sad for members of the Navajo tribe" who were the people primarily

A warning sign posted at a uranium mill in New Mexico warns of possible radioactive contamination. Uranium mill tailings contain 85 percent of the radioactivity found in the original ore.

affected by the mining. A four-part series in the *Los Angeles Times* in November 2006 examined the effects of uranium mining on Navajos in Arizona, New Mexico, and Utah, where 3.9 million tons of uranium ore were extracted from tribal homelands from 1944 to 1986.

The results, as the *Times* put it, were deadly: "The cancer death rate on the reservation historically much lower than that of the general U.S. population—doubled from the early 1970s to the late 1990s, according to Indian Health Service data." And according to the *Times* exposé, the Navajos' exposure was known to the government: "Early on, federal scientists knew that mine workers were at heightened risk for developing lung cancer and other serious respiratory diseases in 15 or 20 years. . . . In 1990, Congress offered the former miners an apology and compensation of up to $150,000 each."

Similar dangers attend to the processing and transportation of nuclear materials, and, most notably and permanently, to nuclear waste. . . .

What next? Weighing the grave risks and harmful effects of nuclear power against the benefits bestowed, it's clear that we're called to a very different path in our response to the dangers of global warming. "Nuclear power is not a solution for climate change," argues Irene Kock of the Nuclear Awareness Project. "It is a cynical gambit on the part of the global nuclear power industry to save itself from being phased out."

No new reactors have been ordered since the accident at Three Mile Island in 1979. If we choose to spend billions on a new generation of nuclear power plants, we not only risk the health and well-being of the American people now and in the future, but we derail the opportunity to jump-start a genuinely green economy that brings healthy and productive manufacturing jobs back into the U.S.

Renewable Energy Is the Answer to the Climate Crisis

The choice before us is not between continuing reliance on fossil fuel or turning back to nuclear power. There is a way forward, a

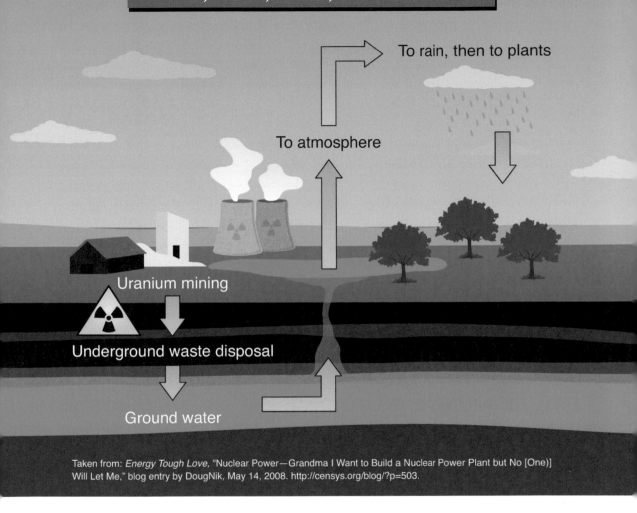

How Nuclear Radiation Moves Through Air, Water, Plants, and Humans

To rain, then to plants

To atmosphere

Uranium mining

Underground waste disposal

Ground water

way that promises not only to cut greenhouse gases and provide enough energy for an expanding world economy, but does so in a manner that encourages democratization, local empowerment, and sustainability.

The way forward is through energy efficiency and renewables, both in local applications and in mass production. A study by Bill Keepin and Gregory Kats, energy analysts at Rocky Mountain Institute in Old Snowmass, Colo., demonstrated that every dollar invested in energy efficiency displaces seven times as much CO_2

emissions as the same dollar invested in nuclear power. Most efficiency improvements are fast and cheap compared to nuclear power, and unlike nuclear, they apply to every kind of energy use, including transportation. And sustainable technologies such as wind power, biomass, geothermal, and especially solar are on the verge of breaking through—despite decades of opposition from the very forces that benefit from large-scale nuclear, coal, and oil energy sources—to the mass production levels needed to meet worldwide energy needs, at an affordable price.

In the final analysis, perhaps Greenpeace founder Patrick Moore was correct. Not in his recent industry-spokesperson persona touting nuclear power as the "environmentally benign" energy source, but rather when he decried the creation of these "dangerous devices" as irresponsible and criminal.

Given how rapidly the symptoms of climate change are becoming manifest in our warming world, and given the fact that our energy choices over the next decade promise to affect our descendents for generations—and the world perhaps even longer than that—it is no exaggeration to say that the human family confronts an epochal fork in the road.

"The future is not a result of choices among alternative paths offered by the present," wrote political theorist John Schaar, "but a place that is created—created first in the mind and will, created next in activity." Such activity, Schaar concludes, "changes both the maker and the destination."

The issue before us is not merely political, or economic, or even scientific. Finally, as the U.S. Catholic bishops put it in their statement on climate change, "It is about our human stewardship of God's creation and our responsibility to those who come after us."

NINE

Nuclear Power Increases the Risk of Nuclear Terrorism

Helen Caldicott

Helen Caldicott is a leading advocate for the antinuclear movement. She received the Lannan Prize for Cultural Freedom in 2003 and has been nominated for the Nobel Peace Prize. She is the author of *If You Love This Planet: A Plan to Save the Earth* and *Nuclear Power Is Not the Answer*. In the following viewpoint Caldicott argues that nuclear power plants are highly vulnerable to terrorist attacks, and that the consequences of such an attack would be catastrophic, potentially killing more than half a million people. According to Caldicott, numerous studies show that nuclear plants are not well enough protected to withstand the type of airborne attacks that occurred in the United States on September 11, 2001. She also suggests that if knowledgeable terrorists gained access to the control panel of a nuclear plant, they could quickly cause a nuclear meltdown, thereby releasing a great deal of deadly radioactivity.

The report of the 9/11 Commission [a government commission set up to report on the circumstances surrounding the terrorist attacks on September 11, 2001] revealed that al Qaeda [the terrorist organization behind the attacks] had considered plans to attack nuclear power plants. The commission thought that scenario was unlikely, however, because of their mistaken belief that the airspace around nuclear power plants was "restricted" and that planes violating that air space would be shot down before impact.

They were wrong. No-fly zones around reactors do not exist on a standard basis, even today [2006]; they are imposed only at times of heightened threat. No surface-to-air missiles are deployed around nuclear power plants. (Many such missiles are deployed around Washington, D.C., however, since 9/11. Evidently, politicians have decided that it is more important to protect their own lives than those of the millions of people who could die lingering, painful deaths after a terrorist-induced nuclear meltdown.

Nuclear Plants Are Vulnerable to an Airborne Attack

According to John Large, a UK [United Kingdom] consulting engineer, in an article in *Global Health Watch*, "Nuclear power plants are almost totally ill-prepared for a terrorist attack from the air" because nuclear reactors were designed and constructed more than fifty years ago, well before the large airplanes in common use today were ever conceived. According to Large, a full-sized passenger plane travelling at great speed with a full load of fuel could significantly damage a nuclear reactor, while injecting large quantities of burning fuel into vulnerable areas of the building. This, in turn, could induce enough damage that a meltdown would occur, leading to the release of large quantities of radiation.

Most nuclear reactors are not required by the NRC [Nuclear Regulatory Commission] to be able to withstand attacks from planes or boats. Large points out that designs of relevant nuclear power plants are easy to obtain in the open literature, and he says that there are no practical measures to take to ensure reactors will not be severely damaged. Others, however, have recommended that the vulnerable aspects of a nuclear power plant could be protected by a series of steel beams set vertically in deep concrete foundations connected with bracing beams, a web of high-strength cables, wires, and netting linking the vertical beams to form a protective screen. This so-called Beamhenge would act to slow down an attacking aircraft, fragmenting it into smaller pieces and dispersing the mass of jet fuel, thereby protecting the vulnerable containment vessel, the spent fuel pool, and other vital pieces of equipment. The NRC has yet to implement any such protective measure.

The external electricity supply to reactors and the emergency diesel generators upon which the safe operation of a nuclear reactor depends are also susceptible to terrorist attack, as is the intake of cooling water from the nearby sea, river, or lake.

Security at Nuclear Plants Is Inadequate

Time magazine recently examined the degree of security available at nuclear power plants post 9/11. Although security at civilian airports has been enormously improved, security at nuclear power plants is virtually unchanged, even though these facilities constitute potential weapons of mass destruction and, as such, are inviting targets for terrorists. In truth, terrorists do not need their own weapons of mass destruction, as such weapons are conveniently deployed all over the world next to large and strategically important populations.

Time magazine opens its article with an attack scenario that goes like this:

> The first hint of trouble probably would be no more than shadows flitting through the darkness outside one of the nation's nuclear reactors. Beyond the fencing, black-clad snipers would take aim at sentries atop guard towers ringing the site. The guards tend to doubt they would be safe in their bullet-resistant enclosures; they call such perches iron coffins, which is what they could become if the terrorists used deadly but easily obtainable .50 caliber sniper rifles.

> The saboteurs would break through fences using bolt cutters or Bangalore torpedoes, pipe-shaped explosives developed by the British in India nearly a century ago. The terrorists would blast through outer walls using platter charges,

directed explosives developed during World War II, giving them access to the heart of the plant. They would use gun-mounted lasers and infra-red devices to blind the plant's cameras, and electronic jammers to paralyze communications among its defenders. They would probably be armed with hand-drawn maps, drawings of control panels, weak spots in the site's defenses provided by a covert comrade working inside the plant.

Once inside the plant with access to the control room they would and could easily flip a few well-learned switches, shutting pumps and operating key valves to cause a deadly loss of coolant. As the nuclear engineer David Lochbaum says, it may sound far-fetched, but "it's irreversible once that last switch is flipped."

The security level at nuclear power plants in the United States has remained essentially unchanged since 9/11.

A Deliberate Meltdown Could Happen Quickly

Many of the scenarios above were taken from a DOE [Department of Energy] training video for guards at nuclear power plants. As Paul Blanch, a nuclear safety expert, writes, "A knowledgeable terrorist inside a control room can cause a meltdown in fairly short order."

The Nuclear Regulatory Commission, in its Design Basis Threat (DBT)—a scenario projecting the maximum threat that nuclear plant security systems are required to protect against—has always insisted that nuclear plants need only be protected against an attack by a maximum of three people outside with the help of one insider. They also have assumed that the attackers would act as a single team and be armed only with hand-held automatic rifles. Now, after 9/11, the NRC requires that guards can protect against up to eight attackers. Yet nineteen highly organized men made the attack on 9/11.

The security guards at nuclear power plants complain of low morale, inadequate training, exhaustion from excessive overtime, and poor pay. They often are expected to work seventy-two hours a week, and not infrequently they go to sleep on the job. They state that they would not be prepared to die to save the reactor, considering their poor compensation and the treatment they routinely receive from management.

The NRC defends the poor state of security at nuclear reactors by saying that a force as large as the 9/11 team constitutes an enemy of the state, rendering the protection of nuclear power plants the job of the Pentagon and the federal government (who would never get to the reactor in time).

Most Simulated Attacks Were Successful

Wackenhut Corporation, the huge security firm contracted to guard half the country's reactors, is the same company that has been contracted to test the security at the reactors. Since, by law, each plant must be tested once every three years, Wackenhut must conduct simulated test attacks an average of twice a month. In 2003, Wackenhut "attackers" tipped off Wackenhut guards about the details of the drill. Wackenhut employee Kathy Davidson at Pilgrim Nuclear Station in Massachusetts was fired from her job because she complained that security was inadequate at the plants. Davidson later told *Time* magazine that, of the twenty-nine classroom exercises Wackenhut conducted to prove that guards could defend against terrorists, the attackers won twenty-eight.

According to Edwin Lyman, a physicist with the Union of Concerned Scientists, a terrorist-induced meltdown could kill more than half-a-million people. Yet Marvin Fertel from the Nuclear Energy Institute, the industry's research institute, continues to insist that only about one hundred people would be killed in such an attack, and the chances of terrorists achieving this goal are "so incredibly low it is not credible."

Congressman Christopher Shays, who chairs the House Reform Committee's panel on national security and emerging threats, believes that the NRC's DBT prediction is artificially low because of economic pressures, amounting to how much security we can afford, not how much we need. Some nuclear security officials call it "the funding basis threat."

A recent [2005] study by the National Academy of Sciences on the dangers posed by terrorists to 43,600 tons of spent fuel stored at the sixty-four power plant sites across the United States concluded that an additional study of security at the nation's nuclear plants is urgently needed.

TEN

Nuclear Power Does Not Increase the Risk of Nuclear Terrorism

Joseph M. Shuster

> Joseph M. Shuster is a chemical engineer, entrepreneur, and businessman and the author of *Beyond Fossil Fools: The Roadmap to Energy Independence by 2040*. In the following viewpoint Shuster argues that the type of fuel used to generate nuclear power is virtually impossible to use to create a working nuclear weapon. He outlines six scenarios that could lead to a rogue nation or a terrorist group acquiring a nuclear weapon and explains why he thinks using fuel from a nuclear power plant would be the most difficult and unsuccessful method of creating a usable bomb, especially for a subnational group. For example, he says, the material is quite heavy and radioactive, making it easy to detect and extremely difficult to transport or handle. Building and operating nuclear power plants, he says, does not substantially increase the risk of nuclear terrorism.

Can Rogue Nations and Terrorists Make Weapons from Nuclear Material Used to Generate Energy? The short answer is an emphatic no. The long answer is no, no, no. It would be infinitely easier to acquire a credible nuclear weapon by buying one on the black market or by buying or stealing some Plutonium-239 than to try to make a bomb from reactor-grade waste, particularly the waste from a fast neutron reactor. The crucially essential point: *Reactor-grade* material is not the same as *weapons-grade* material.

To be sure, many glaring, troubling proliferation problems exist, but managing the spent fuel from power reactors is not one of them. Creating weapons-grade Plutonium-239 is a fairly detectable and expensive endeavor. . . .

Whether new nuclear power plants are built or not, any nation with reasonable technical capabilities and adequate resources can make a nuclear bomb, and there is nothing the United States or any other nation can do about it except exert political pressure or military action. . . .

Rogue Nations

Since nations have considerable financial and technical resources, they could acquire the means to build a nuclear weapon. The effort is expensive and requires non-trivial inter-disciplinary technical skills. Let's see how *nations*, especially rogue nations, could acquire nuclear weapons, listed in order of possible success.

1. *Steal or buy a nuclear weapon.* This is not easy because of security, size, and weight. Such a weapon would likely be detected in transit. The smallest weighs approximately one-half ton, but most are much larger. A stolen bomb probably could not be detonated because of built-in safeguards. However, if a nation had the requisite technical capability, the stolen weapon could possibly be disassembled and reassembled to work.

2. *Buy or steal highly enriched uranium or weapons-grade Plutonium-239.* This is a troubling prospect because so much of this stuff sits around the world. Numerous reports suggest some of this material has already been sold clandestinely, much of it from Russia shortly after the collapse of the Soviet Union. Of course, after acquiring such material, one still faces the non-trivial task of fabricating a usable weapon.

3. *Buy uranium ore and equipment to enrich the content of Uranium-235 to a concentration sufficient for bomb-making, and employ many scientists in various disciplines to fabricate a bomb.* They don't need a nuclear reactor, but they do need considerable money and technical talent to be successful.

4. *Build a light-water reactor and use it to make weapons-grade Plutonium-239.* Run the reactor for short periods of time (30–60 days), then extract and concentrate the Plutonium-239 until one has enough to fabricate a bomb. The longer the reactor runs, the more the Plutonium-239 is subjected to neutron bombardment. The more bombardment, the heavier the plutonium becomes, converting to Plutonium-240, then Plutonium-241, then Plutonium-242. These isotopes are lousy for making a bomb. Also, a nation would still need significant financial and technical resources to fabricate a nuclear weapon.

5. *Steal, buy, or use "waste" (used, spent fuel) from a light-water reactor. . . .* This nasty material is easily detected and difficult to handle and transport. The spent fuel is very radioactive and is in 6- to 12-foot rods weighing hundreds of pounds each. Only an idiot would try to use it to make a weapon, even though theoretically one might be able to make a low-grade device if the builder doesn't fatally irradiate or otherwise kill himself in the process. For the danger and effort, the almost certain result would be the construction of a weapon that won't work.

6. *Steal, buy, or use some fuel or waste from a fast neutron reactor.* If creating a nuclear weapon from spent fuel from a light-water reactor is essentially impossible, then doing so with the recycled fuel from a fast neutron reactor is doubly impossible because the fuel is much more radioactive. Also, the waste material from a fast neutron reactor contains only the faintest, trace amounts of plutonium, so serves no purpose as a weapons component.

Shown here is a nuclear fuel pellet. Pellets are used to power nuclear reactors; however, they cannot be used to produce nuclear weapons.

Only the first four possibilities listed above are conceivably viable paths to making nuclear weapons.

Terrorists Are Extremely Unlikely to Acquire Nuclear Weapons

While just about any nation could build a nuclear weapon, it would be extremely difficult for any terrorist group to acquire or steal weapon-making materials and then fabricate a workable weapon. Although there is a *remote possibility* that a terrorist group could acquire a bomb, bomb-grade uranium, or plutonium, and then devise a weapon, it is virtually impossible for them to access reactor-grade material and fabricate a credible weapon.

The 6 scenarios above apply. However, scenarios 3 and 4 seem out of reach for terrorist groups, either economically, technically, or both. Also, terrorist groups confront the added burden of detection and interdiction. Scenarios 1 and 2 above seem the most reasonable for a terrorist group, but the daunting task of actually making a usable weapon and the strong possibility of detection are formidable deterrents. Scenarios 5 and 6 above—making a nuclear weapon from spent fuel and nuclear-plant waste—offer no hope for a terrorist group, and only fools would try. Besides, there are easier ways to destroy life.

There is only a small, scant possibility that a sub-national or terrorist group—even one as well organized and financially well-to-do as al-Qaida [the terrorist group responsible for the attacks on Sept 11, 2001 (9/11)]—could develop its own nuclear weapons without a lot of outside help in obtaining the necessary nuclear material and the necessary technologies to fabricate the device and still avoid detection. However, to repeat, there exists a remote risk of well-organized terrorist groups somehow acquiring a fully assembled nuclear weapon from a friendly nuclear state or somehow acquiring sufficient weapons-grade material to significantly reduce the barrier to making one. . . .

Building more nuclear power plants will not make the proliferation issue any worse since the opportunities to make a bomb cited above already exist all over the world.

Dirty Bombs

A dirty bomb, sometimes called a *radiological dispersal device* (RDD), refers to a bomb that combines some radioactive material with a natural explosive to create a device designed to disperse radioactive material over a large area. Since the attacks of 9/11 on New York City and Washington, D.C., many people around the world have been worried about such a bomb. However, a dirty bomb is unlikely to cause many deaths, except for those deaths from the initial conventional explosion. In fact, in the 1960s the U.K. [United Kingdom] Ministry of Defense decided that using conventional explosives in place of

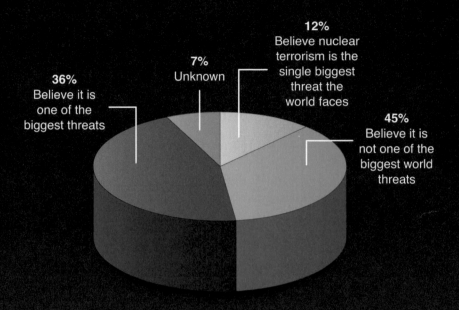

12%
Believe nuclear terrorism is the single biggest threat the world faces

7%
Unknown

36%
Believe it is one of the biggest threats

45%
Believe it is not one of the biggest world threats

Taken from: ABC News, *Political Punch*, "On Nuclear Terrorism a Muted Perception of Threat," blog entry by Gary Langer, April 12, 2010. http://blogs.abcnews.com/thenumbers/2010/04/on-nuclear-terrorism-a-muted-perception-of-threat.html. Source: ABC News/*Washington Post* poll.

radioactive material would be more destructive. Nevertheless, the prospect of a dirty bomb and radioactive exposure causes great fear, perhaps its greatest threat.

Radioactive material for a RDD could come from millions of sources used for medical and industrial purposes around the world. Reactor-grade radioactive material would be the most difficult to acquire, because of its size, inherent properties, and accompanying security systems.

To build a RDD, handlers must overcome many logistical hurdles. The material must be sufficiently radioactive, the material must be safely transportable, and the material must be dispersible. Satisfying all three requirements is difficult. In any case, assembling and transporting a RDD bomb without severe radiation damage and possible death to the perpetrators would be extremely difficult, too. For example, if the radioactive material were properly shielded to prevent contamination during assembly and transport, then the bomb would be very difficult to transport, easier to detect, and much less effective if detonated. If the material were not shielded, then transporting the material and assembling a weapon would be very difficult before the handlers succumbed to radiation sickness and perhaps death.

No radioactive dirty bomb has ever been detonated, although some groups have assembled lethal *chemical* weapons. Since the world has no experience to draw upon, many fear the unknown. However, the experiences at Chernobyl, [the Soviet Union site of the worst nuclear accident in history, in 1986] the experiences at some accidents involving radioactive material, and the results of several analyses indicate that RDDs will neither sicken nor kill many people.

ELEVEN

Nuclear Waste Is a Serious Problem

Greenpeace

> Greenpeace is an independent global campaigning organization that aims to change attitudes and behavior; to protect and conserve the environment; and to promote peace through research, lobbying, and direct acts of resistance against governments and corporations. In the following viewpoint the author argues that nuclear waste remains dangerously radioactive for hundreds of thousands of years and that no effective way of dealing with it has been developed. Greenpeace supports its argument by giving numerous examples of failed attempts to deal with the problem, including the Yucca Mountain site near Las Vegas, Nevada, which had to be abandoned after decades of development and testing as a long-term nuclear waste disposal site when a fault line was discovered in the area.

For over 50 years the nuclear industry has produced large volumes of hazardous radioactive waste along the whole nuclear chain—from uranium mining and enrichment to reactor operation, waste reprocessing and decommissioning. Today, nuclear energy is being sold to politicians and consumers as one of the options for fighting climate change that will also deliver energy security. However, nuclear energy is a dangerous obstacle on the road to a clean energy future. On top of other substantial problems related to safety and costs, nuclear waste remains a major flaw of nuclear energy.

The International Atomic Energy Agency (IAEA) estimates that the industry annually produces 1 million barrels (200,000 m³) [1 cubic meter (m³) equals about 35 cubic feet] of what it considers 'low and intermediate-level waste' and about 50,000 barrels (10,000 m³) of the even more dangerous 'high-level waste'. These numbers do not include spent nuclear fuel, which is also high-level waste.

It takes 240,000 years for radioactive plutonium to decay to a level that is safe for human exposure, which is an even longer period than modern humans have been on the Earth (200,000 years). There is no way to guarantee that these substances can be kept safe for this amount of time. It is senseless to allow the nuclear industry to continue producing more nuclear waste.

Failed Solutions

Billions of euros have been spent over the past half-century on finding a solution to the nuclear waste problem. The attempts have all been unsuccessful.

For years, low level radioactive waste was dumped at sea, 'out of sight and out of mind'. Disintegrating barrels brought the waste back into the environment and dangerous substances accumulated in the bodies of animals. After 15 years of campaigning by Greenpeace, an international treaty was signed in 1993 banning all dumping of radioactive waste at sea.

In Asse, Germany, an experimental radioactive waste dump was set up in the 1960s in salt formations deep underground. A few years ago it was discovered that it had started leaking water in 1988 and is currently flooding with 12,000 litres of water each day. As a result, all 126,000 barrels of waste already placed in the dump now need to be cleared out. Asse was envisaged as a pilot project for a final storage solution in the salt layers under Gorleben, but there is now serious doubt in Germany about the viability of salt layers as storage for nuclear waste.

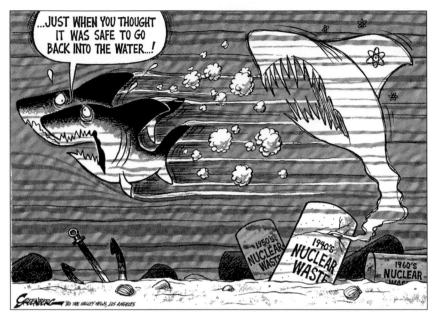

Steve Greenberg, greenberg-art.com, http://www.greenberg-art.com/toons, August 22, 1980.

One of the largest nuclear dumps in the world, the Centre de Stockage de La Manche (CSM) in northern France was opened in 1969 to store low-level waste. It was closed in 1994. It currently stores 520,000 m³ of radioactive materials from waste reprocessing and French nuclear reactors. A 1996 commission set up by the French government concluded that the site also contained long-living waste and high-level waste, and that the true inventory was effectively unknown. In 2006 it was found that contaminated water from the site had already been leaking into an underground aquifer, threatening the surrounding agricultural land.

In 1987, Yucca Mountain—about 80 miles north of Las Vegas—was designated as the site for long-term disposal of radioactive wastes in the United States. However, the US Geological Survey has found a seismic fault line under the site and there are serious doubts about the long-term movements of underground water that can transport deadly contamination into the environment. As a result of these problems and billions of dollars in cost overruns, the US government stopped funding the project in early 2010.

New Research Brings New Challenges

Sweden plans to pack waste in cast iron inserts in copper canisters and place them in holes bored in tunnel floors, deep underground (400–500 metres), surrounded by bentonite clay. Water is expected to make the bentonite clay expand so that it fills the cavities in the surrounding granite rock which would reduce groundwater movement.

Finland adopted the same system and Switzerland and the UK are considering this option. But there are already major concerns. The copper canisters were expected to survive corrosion for at least 100,000 years but recent research shows that they can fail in just 1,000 years or less. There are also concerns about the build-up of hydrogen produced as a result of corrosion. High temperatures from the canisters could also affect the clay buffer, while groundwater flows could bring contaminants from any compromised containers into the biosphere. Furthermore, Nordic countries will face at least one Ice Age in the coming 100,000 years, entailing extremely violent earthquakes, penetration of permafrost to the disposal depth and below, potential intrusion of water and unpredictable changes in groundwater flows.

Unlike Sweden and Finland, which rely on man-made barriers to prevent leakage, France and Belgium are exploring clay as a natural barrier. The waste is to be contained in simple stainless steel canisters, which can corrode much faster than the Swedish copper ones. Hence the French/Belgium concept relies on the natural clay formation to contain radioactivity. The crucial question is whether it can be guaranteed—for hundreds of thousands of years—that no cracks or channels will form in the clay layers, which would cause water to leak in and out again, poisoning nearby aquifers. . . .

The Human Risk of Storage

Human interference. Once placed into final storage, nuclear waste also needs to be monitored and secured from human interference as well as natural events. Stored civilian and military nuclear waste, such as plutonium or uranium, are sources of radioactive material that can be used for the production of nuclear bombs. A few kilograms of these substances would be sufficient to make bombs similar to the ones used on Japan during World War II. Even a very modest amount of radioactive material from waste storage sites would be sufficient to make a 'dirty bomb', which could contaminate an entire city. To deal with the problem, the nuclear industry proposes, at the very best, to guard storage sites for 300 years. But there is no proposal to ensure security for the other 239,700 years. . . .

Interim storage: leakage and terrorist risk. Some countries, like the Netherlands, have set up interim storage for 100 years to safeguard the dangerous waste for a definite period of time. In the meantime, leakages and accidents need to be prevented. The large amounts of highly radioactive waste in storage could lead to massive contamination in the event of failure of the containers or the buildings themselves, either through deterioration or due to external events such as natural disasters (earthquakes, flooding) or malevolent acts. While the nuclear waste debate focuses on final storage, most spent nuclear fuel remains in poorly safeguarded interim storage for decades to come; addressing the flaws in intermediate storage should be the first priority. . . .

Transport of nuclear waste. Nuclear waste, such as spent nuclear fuel, plutonium and other highly radioactive material, is transported all over the planet, often passing through large inhabited areas. These deadly convoys pose a serious risk to populations and ecosystems along the routes. If an accident were to occur, radioactivity could contaminate several square kilometres or more. The convoys are also at risk of terrorist attack. Nuclear transports are regularly met with huge protests because of the risks and the lack of a solution to deal with the dangerous waste. The annual transport of nuclear waste from France to Gorleben in Germany draws tens of thousands of demonstrators. Tonnes of plutonium resulting from reprocessing are also regularly shipped from France and the UK to Japan, crossing the territorial waters

A train loaded with nuclear waste crosses Europe. Transportation of nuclear waste could pose a serious threat to populations, were accidents to happen during transport.

of many countries on the way, as well as important marine eco-systems. Depleted uranium from Europe has been transported to Russia, where thousands of barrels are dumped in large open-air storage sites in the Urals.

TWELVE

Nuclear Waste Is an Easily Managed Problem

World Nuclear Association

The World Nuclear Association is an international organization that promotes nuclear energy and supports the many companies that comprise the global nuclear industry. In the following viewpoint the author argues that nuclear waste is an easily managed problem using established technologies and practices. The author notes that the amount of waste produced by the nuclear power industry is less than 1 percent of the total amount of industrial toxic waste. The World Nuclear Association also points out that whereas nonnuclear waste remains toxic forever, nuclear waste becomes progressively less radioactive over time, so that after about fifty years it is only 1/1000th as radioactive as when it was first produced.

All parts of the nuclear fuel cycle produce some radioactive waste (radwaste) and the cost of managing and disposing of this is part of the electricity cost, *i.e.* it is internalised and paid for by the electricity consumers.

At each stage of the fuel cycle there are proven technologies to dispose of the radioactive wastes safely. For low- and intermediate-level wastes these are mostly being implemented. For high-level wastes some countries await the accumulation of enough of it to

World Nuclear Association, "Radioactive Waste Management," June 2009. www.world-nuclear.org. Reproduced by permission.

warrant building geological repositories; others, such as the USA, have encountered political delays.

The radioactivity of all nuclear waste decays with time. Each radionuclide [radioactive forms of elements] contained in the waste has a half-life—the time taken for half of its atoms to decay and thus for it to lose half of its radioactivity. . . . Eventually all radioactive wastes decay into non-radioactive elements. The more radioactive an isotope is, the faster it decays.

The main objective in managing and disposing of radioactive (or other) waste is to protect people and the environment. This means isolating or diluting the waste so that the rate or concentration of any radionuclides returned to the biosphere is harmless. To achieve this, practically all wastes are contained and managed—some clearly need deep and permanent burial. From nuclear power generation, none is allowed to cause harmful pollution.

All toxic wastes need to be dealt with safely, not just radioactive wastes. In countries with nuclear power, radioactive wastes comprise less than 1% of total industrial toxic wastes (the balance of which remains hazardous indefinitely).

Types of Radioactive Wastes

Exempt waste & very low level waste. Exempt waste and very low level waste (VLLW) contains radioactive materials at a level which is not considered harmful to people or the surrounding environment. It consists mainly of demolished material (such as concrete, plaster, bricks, metal, valves, piping, *etc.*) produced during rehabilitation or dismantling operations on nuclear industrial sites. Other industries, such as food processing, chemical, steel *etc* also produce VLLW as a result of the concentration of natural radioactivity present in certain minerals used in their manufacturing processes. . . . The waste is therefore disposed of with domestic refuse, although countries such as France are currently developing facilities to store VLLW in specifically designed VLLW disposal facilities.

Decay in Radioactivity of Fission Products in One Tonne of Spent Fuel

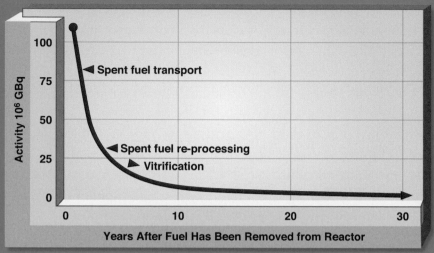

GBq = 10^9 becquerel [1 becquerel = levent of radiation emission per second]
Source: Cogema

Taken from: World Nuclear Association, "Radioactive Waste Management," June 2009. www.world-nuclear.org/info/inf0.html.

Major Low-Level Radioactive Waste Disposal Sites

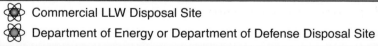

Taken from: US Environmental Protection Agency, "Low-Level Radioactive Waste," October 4, 2007. www.epa.gov/rpdweb00/radwaste/402-k-94-001-llw.html.

Low-level waste. Low-level waste (LLW) is generated from hospitals and industry, as well as the nuclear fuel cycle. It comprises paper, rags, tools, clothing, filters *etc*, which contain small amounts of mostly short-lived radioactivity. It does not require shielding during handling and transport and is suitable for shallow land burial. To reduce its volume, it is often compacted or incinerated before disposal. It comprises some 90% of the volume but only 1% of the radioactivity of all radioactive waste.

Intermediate-level waste. Intermediate-level waste (ILW) contains higher amounts of radioactivity and some requires shielding. It typically comprises resins, chemical sludges and metal fuel cladding, as well as contaminated materials from reactor decommissioning. Smaller items and any non-solids may be solidified in concrete or bitumen for disposal. It makes up some 7% of the volume and has 4% of the radioactivity of all radwaste.

High-level waste. High-level waste (HLW) arises from the 'burning' of uranium fuel in a nuclear reactor. HLW contains the fission products and transuranic elements generated in the reactor core. It is highly radioactive and hot, so requires cooling and shielding. It can be considered as the 'ash' from 'burning' uranium. HLW accounts for over 95% of the total radioactivity produced in the process of electricity generation. . . .

As already noted, the volume of nuclear waste produced by the nuclear industry is very small compared with other wastes generated. . . .

A typical 1000 MWe [megawatt, 1 million watts] light water reactor will generate (directly and indirectly) 200–350 m^3 low- and intermediate-level waste per year. It will also discharge about 20 m^3 (27 tonnes) of used fuel per year, which corresponds to a 75 m^3 disposal volume following encapsulation if it is treated as waste. Where that used fuel is reprocessed, only 3 m^3 of vitrified waste (glass) is produced, which is equivalent to a 28 m^3 disposal volume following placement in a disposal canister.

This compares with an average 400,000 tonnes of ash produced from a coal-fired plant of the same power capacity. Today, volume reduction techniques and abatement technologies as well as continuing good practice within the work force all contribute to continuing minimisation of waste produced, a key principle of waste management policy in the nuclear industry. Whilst the volumes of nuclear wastes produced are very small, the most important issue for the nuclear industry is managing their toxic nature in a way that is environmentally sound and presents no hazard to both workers and the general public.

Managing HLW from Used Fuel

Used fuel gives rise to HLW which may be either the used fuel itself in fuel rods, or the separated waste arising from reprocessing this. In either case, the amount is modest—as noted above, a typical reactor generates about 27 tonnes of spent fuel or 3 m^3 per year of vitrified waste. Both can be effectively and economically isolated, and have been handled and stored safely since nuclear power began.

Storage is mostly in ponds at reactor sites, or occasionally at a central site. Some 90% of the world's used fuel is stored thus and some of it has been there for decades. The ponds are usually about seven metres deep, to allow three metres of water over the used fuel to fully shield it. The water also cools it. Some storage is in dry casks or vaults with air circulation and the fuel is surrounded by concrete.

If the used fuel is reprocessed, as is that from UK [United Kingdom], French, Japanese and German reactors, HLW comprises highly-radioactive fission products and some transuranic elements with long-lived radioactivity. These are separated from the used fuel, enabling the uranium and plutonium to be recycled. Liquid HLW from reprocessing must be solidified. The HLW also generates a considerable amount of heat and requires cooling. It is vitrified into borosilicate (Pyrex) glass, encapsulated into heavy stainless steel cylinders about 1.3 metres high and stored for eventual disposal deep underground. This material has no conceivable future use and is unequivocally waste. . . .

If used reactor fuel is not reprocessed, it will still contain all the highly radioactive isotopes, . . . since it largely consists of uranium (with a little plutonium), it represents a potentially valu-

Nuclear fuel waste is held in pools at a storage facility in France. Ninety percent of the world's spent nuclear fuel is stored in pools at reactor sites.

able resource and there is an increasing reluctance to dispose of it irretrievably.

Either way, after 40–50 years the heat and radioactivity have fallen to one thousandth of the level at removal. This provides a technical incentive to delay further action with HLW until the radioactivity has reduced to about 0.1% of its original level.

After storage for about 40 years the used fuel assemblies are ready for encapsulation or loading into casks ready for indefinite storage or permanent disposal underground.

Direct disposal of used fuel has been chosen by the USA and Sweden among others, although evolving concepts lean towards making it recoverable if future generations see it as a resource. This means allowing for a period of management and oversight before a repository is closed.

THIRTEEN

Nuclear Waste Is a Valuable Resource

Marjorie Mazel Hecht

Marjorie Mazel Hecht is a writer for *21st Century Science and Technology*, a quarterly magazine dedicated to the promotion of continual scientific progress. In the following viewpoint Hecht argues that spent nuclear fuel, far from being a waste product, is actually a valuable resource. She claims that the used fuel can be recycled and used again to produce more nuclear power, noting that "the spent fuel produced by a single 1,000-megawatt nuclear plant over its forty-year lifetime is equal to the energy in 5 billion gallons of oil." In addition, she notes that there are elements in the waste that have applications ranging from medical devices to smoke detectors and much more, including applications that will be developed in the future.

There's no such thing as *nuclear waste*! This nasty term was invented just to stop the development of civilian nuclear power.

The spent fuel from nuclear power plants is actually a precious resource: About 96% of it can be recycled into new nuclear fuel. No other fuel source can make this claim—wood, coal, oil, or gas. Once these fuels are burned, all that's left is some ash or airborne pollutant by-products, which nuclear energy does not produce.

Thus, nuclear is a truly *renewable* resource. Furthermore, unlike wind, solar, and other so-called alternative energy sources, a nuclear fission reactor (the fast reactor or breeder reactor) can actually *create more fuel* than it uses up.

Atoms for Peace

In the Atoms for Peace days of the 1950s and 1960s, it was assumed that spent reactor fuel would be reprocessed into new reactor fuel. The initial plan was for the United States and other nuclear

Recycled nuclear fuel is unloaded in Japan. Of the spent nuclear fuel now being stored, 96 percent can be recycled—which is not the case for all other types of fuel.

nations to have closed nuclear fuel cycles, not "once-through" cycles. In the closed fuel cycle, uranium is mined, enriched, and processed into fuel rods; then it is burned as fuel and reprocessed, to start the cycle again.

"Burying" spent fuel (as planned for Yucca Mountain) was not in the Atoms for Peace picture. Why bury a fuel source that could provide thousands of metric tons of uranium-238, fissile uranium-235, and plutonium-239 that could be used to make new reactor fuel?

But . . . the U.S. stopped its reprocessing program in the 1970s and instead now stores spent nuclear fuel, waiting for a long-term burial site. Despite the scary headlines, the total amount of spent fuel in storage in the United States is small. The U.S. Department of Energy stated in 2007: "If we were to take all the spent fuel produced to date in the United States and stack it side-by-side, end-to-end, the fuel assemblies would cover an area about the size of a football field to a depth of about five yards."

The amount of usable fuel in that hypothetical football field, however, is vast. Burying 70,000 metric tons of spent nuclear fuel would waste 66,000 metric tons of uranium-238, which could be used to make new fuel, and an additional 1,200 metric tons of fissile uranium-235 and plutonium-239, the energetic part of the fuel mixture. Looking at it another way, the spent fuel produced by a single 1,000-megawatt nuclear plant over its 40-year lifetime is equal to the energy in 5 billion gallons of oil, or 37 million tons of coal. Would you throw that away?

Medical Applications for Nuclear Waste

In addition to the multi-trillion-dollar amount of new reactor fuel that could be recycled from 96% of the spent nuclear fuel now in storage, the remaining 4% of so-called high-level waste—about 2,500 metric tons—is also usable. Dr. Michael Fox, a physical chemist and nuclear engineer, has estimated that there are about 80 tons each of cesium-137 and strontium-90 that could be separated out for use in medical applications, such as targetted radioisotope therapies, or sterilization of equipment.

Using isotope separation techniques, and fast-neutron bombardment for transmutation (technologies that the United States has refused to develop), we could separate out other valuable radioisotopes, like americium, which is widely used in smoke detectors, or plutonium-238, which is used to power heart pacemakers, as well as small reactors in space. Krypton-85, tritium, and promethium-147 are used in self-powered lights in remote applications; strontium-90 is used to provide electric power for remote weather stations, and in remote surveillance stations, navigational aids, and defense communications systems. . . .

Every Problem Has a Solution

Nobody likes "waste." . . . Environmentalists today have a fixation on "waste," because to them it represents "evil" industrialized

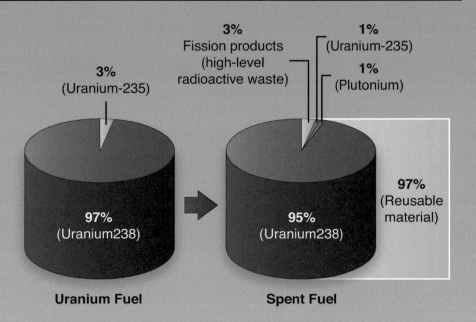

Amount of Reusable Fuel in a Spent (Used) Fuel Rod

3%
(Uranium-235)

97%
(Uranium238)

Uranium Fuel

3%
Fission products
(high-level
radioactive waste)

1%
(Uranium-235)

1%
(Plutonium)

95%
(Uranium238)

97%
(Reusable
material)

Spent Fuel

Taken from: *Cool Hand Nuke,* "A Blue Ribbon Commission Will Hold Its First Meeting March 25–26 in Washington, DC," blog entry by Dan, March 6, 2010. www.coolhandnuke.com/cool-hand-blog/ArticleID/35/The-future-of-spent-nuclear-fuel.aspx.

civilization. Human beings are measured in terms of how much solid waste they produce each year. In the United States, the "Environmental Almanac" solemnly warns, each American creates three-quarters of a ton of solid waste yearly! The obvious solution is to stop looking at the wrong end of the human being. Instead, focus on the head, and how the human mind can invent new solutions to problems!

Here are some of the solutions:

We know how to reprocess used nuclear fuel, and can do it safely, as this country did for years. We also know that there are new technologies to be developed that can eliminate the long-lived radioisotopes in the 4% of used nuclear fuel that cannot be recycled. New technologies could retrieve many of these isotopes for use in medicine and industry.

We can develop fusion power, with high enough temperatures (millions of degrees) to reduce nuclear spent fuel and other matter—including garbage or rock—down to its constituent elements. The fusion torch was an idea patented in the 1960s, but its development was stopped by . . . anti-nuclear forces. . . . Plasma torches, with lower than fusion temperatures, are used today in industry in several applications—steelmaking, for example.

The idea here, absent from the green mentality, is that advanced technologies should be used to eliminate pollution. For every problem there is a solution.

The anti-nukes know that reprocessing is possible. Their next argument is "safety." They assume that human beings are not capable of using advanced technologies safely. Of course, all of life is risky, and it is through human beings' creative ability that we design ways to protect ourselves from danger. Again, the anti-nukes' argument looks at the wrong end of the human being.

But then comes the argument: "What about terrorism? What if bad people get hold of nuclear materials?" The United States successfully reprocessed spent nuclear fuel in the past, in a secure fashion. We can do it again.

"Ah, but it costs too much," the learned anti-nukes of the Union of Concerned Scientists, among others, then say. They produce an accountant's balance sheet of costs and benefits to show that it's cheaper *not* to reprocess. Left out of this accountant's argument, however, is reality. We are not going to get out of civilization's most catastrophic financial collapse unless we massively invest now in the infrastructure projects, including nuclear power plants, that will guarantee adequate power for future generations. Not doing that will kill people. The cost/benefit accountant's mentality is a death trap.

FOURTEEN

France Is a Nuclear Power Success Story

Alan M. Herbst and George W. Hopley

Alan M. Herbst has an master's degree in finance and international business from the Stern School of Business and twenty years' experience in energy consulting. George W. Hopley is associate director of commodity research at the investment bank Barclays Capital and previously served as senior director of research and analysis for Duke Energy. In the following viewpoint Herbst and Hopley argue that America can learn from the highly successful French nuclear power industry, which supplies almost 80 percent of that country's electricity needs. According to the authors, France was motivated to pursue nuclear energy to lessen its dependence on foreign oil. Cultural factors, such as a desire for independence and trust in scientists and engineers, helped overcome people's fear of nuclear radiation, and intelligent management of the industry, for example using one standard nuclear reactor design, allowed the industry to quickly and efficiently grow to supply most of the country's energy needs.

While nuclear power is a contentious issue in the United States, it has greater acceptance internationally, especially in France. To many nuclear energy proponents, France is a bea-

Alan M. Herbst and George W. Hopley, "Nuclear Power's Growing Global Footprint," *Nuclear Energy Now*. John Wiley & Sons, 2007. Copyright © 2007 by Alan M. Herbst and George W. Hopley. All rights reserved. This material is used by permission of John Wiley & Sons, Inc.

con for the nuclear power industry. The first French commercial nuclear power plant was commissioned in 1963; since then the nation has built an impressive and yet relatively young group of reactors. . . .

Over the past half-century, the French have overcome many of the same issues and challenges that face the U.S. nuclear industry today. These include regulatory oversight, waste disposal, and safety concerns. The French, motivated through their desire to remain energy independent, successfully met these challenges, thereby enabling their heavy reliance on nuclear energy. . . .

France has 59 nuclear reactors. These are operated by Electricite de France (EdF) and have a total capacity of over 63 gigawatts, supplying over 426 billion kilowatt-hours per year of electricity. France has the second-largest electricity sector in the European Union [EU], behind Germany. In 2005, French electricity generation was 549 billion kilowatt-hours net and consumption was 482 billion kilowatt-hours, or 7,700 kilowatt-hours per person. The country depends on nuclear energy for almost 80 percent of its electricity. This figure is approximately four times greater than the percentage of electricity generated by nuclear power in the United States and approximately twice the percentage of electricity generated by Sweden, its closest nuclear generation competitor in Europe.

France's increased use of nuclear energy, has also helped curtail its dependence on imported oil and has had a dramatic effect on the amount of greenhouse gas emissions produced. France produces electricity more economically than other European countries and has become the largest net exporter of electricity in the EU. . . .

France is the world's largest nuclear power generator on a per capita basis and ranks second in total installed nuclear capacity behind the United States. Its ascent to its relative position of dominance in the field of generation was not by chance, but the result of a well-orchestrated effort on behalf of the French government.

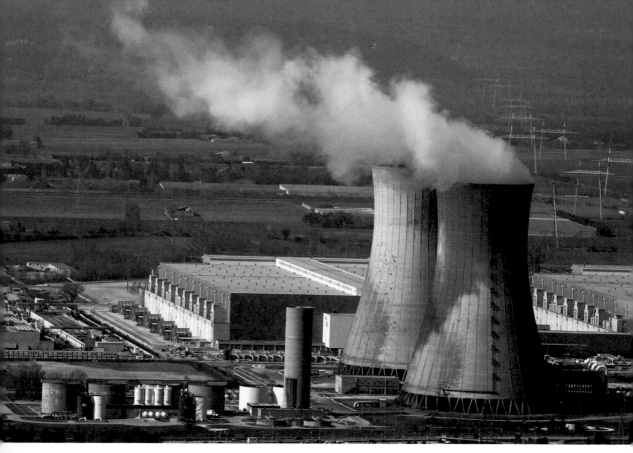

A view of the Tricastin nuclear power plant located in Pierrelatte, France. Thus far, the French have built fifty-nine nuclear reactors that generate over 426 billion kilowatt hours of electricity per year.

The Drivers Behind French Commercial Nuclear Development

France does not possess any sizable deposits of fossil fuels, and it relied mostly on imported oil to run its growing post–World War II economy. The French realized just how dependent and vulnerable their economy was to imported Middle East oil in 1956 when Egypt, after nationalizing the waterway, blocked transit through the Suez Canal, a major transit route for oil from the Middle East to Europe. The French government's fears were realized again less than two decades later, in 1973, with the effects of a global Arab oil embargo. To lessen their dependence on foreign sources of fossil fuels, the French enacted an ambitious nuclear power building program that called for the construction of six reactors per year. The national rallying cry for this initiative was the slogan, "France doesn't have oil, but it has ideas." . . .

The French nuclear program is based on American technology. After experimenting with gas-cooled reactors in the 1960s, the French gave up and purchased American pressurized water reactors designed by Westinghouse. By purchasing just one type of reactor, the French were able to build their plants more economically than nuclear facilities built in the United States. Moreover, management of safety was much easier since the lessons learned from an incident at one nuclear facility could be quickly implemented by managers at another identical French reactor. This centralized planning and management have been critical to the success of France's nuclear industry, enabling it to operate safely and efficiently. . . .

Why Nuclear Energy Works in France

How was France able to get its people to accept nuclear power when the citizens of other nations, especially the United States, have been so hostile to the concept? What can nuclear project developers learn from the French experience? The answer to the first question can be explained by the uniqueness of French culture and politics.

First, the French tend to place a high value on their independence as a nation. While this at times might make them a problematic ally (from the U.S. government's point of view) it has greatly benefited their nuclear industry development. To the French, the thought of being dependent on the volatile Middle East for their energy was quite disturbing. French citizens, perhaps sensing their diminished role as a superpower on the post–World War II stage, quickly accepted the notion that nuclear power might be a necessity since they, in their diminished role, could not adequately secure or protect their supply of imported oil. A popular French slogan at the time, "No oil, no gas, no coal, no choice," succinctly sums up their position. . . .

The success of nuclear energy in France has a lot to do with French culture. The French have a history of large, centrally managed technology projects that have been extremely popular with the public. The public's mostly positive response to the development of nuclear energy appears to follow the same pattern as its approval of the costly development of high-speed bullet trains and supersonic passenger jets. Part of the popularity of these large government projects probably stems from the fact that in France, scientists and engineers tend to have a higher status than in the United States and that many high-ranking French civil servants and government officials are trained as scientists and engineers,

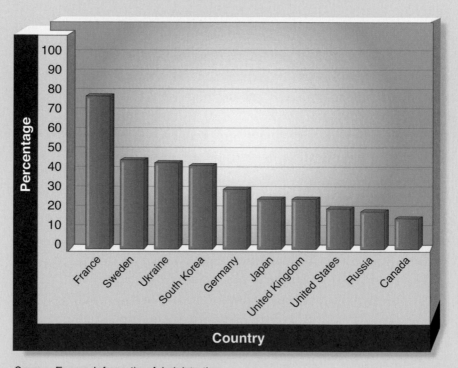

Nuclear Power as a Percentage of Electricity Generation

Source: Energy Information Administration.

Taken from: Alan M. Herbst and George W. Hopley, *Nuclear Energy Now*, Hoboken; Wiley, 2007, p. 96.

rather than lawyers as in the United States. The engineering experience of these French technocrats led them to develop a highly standardized, centrally planned nuclear industry that encourages efficiencies in training and operations. This has also contributed to the overall safety of the French nuclear industry.

Lastly, French authorities have worked hard to highlight the benefits of nuclear energy as well as the risks. Multimillion-dollar television advertising campaigns were implemented to reinforce the link between nuclear power and the electricity used by consumers. French nuclear plants also solicited the public to take tours, an invitation that 6 million Frenchman accepted, although this policy is probably a thing of the past due to recent concerns over the security of such installations.

French public opinion polls at times have shown that approximately two-thirds of the population is strongly in favor of nuclear power. While French people have similar negative imagery and fears of radiation and disaster as Americans, the difference is that cultural, economic, and political forces in France appear to counteract these fears. French citizens cannot control nuclear technology any more than Americans can, but the fact that they trust their technocrats who do control it makes them feel more secure. Most French people know that life would be very difficult without nuclear energy.

FIFTEEN

France Is Not a Nuclear Power Success Story

SpaceDaily

Space Daily is an online news site providing news related to space exploration, earth science, energy technology, and other topics. In the following viewpoint the authors claim that the French nuclear power industry is in serious crisis. They base this assessment on a 2010 report by Mark Cooper that details a number of issues the industry faces both in France and also in the United States. According to the report, both countries have experienced dramatic cost increases in the nuclear industry since the early 1970s. Also, in France the heavy reliance on nuclear power has resulted in less emphasis on renewable energy and energy efficiency—a pattern the authors say is also true of US states that have pursued nuclear power. The authors argue that the French nuclear power industry is not a success story, and that the United States should not follow their example.

The so-called "French nuclear miracle" embraced by some U.S. policymakers as a model for this nation is a misconception masking a pattern of fast-rising nuclear reactor construction costs and a "crowding out" of investments in renewable energy, such as wind, solar and hydro-electric power, according to a new study by Vermont Law School's [VLS] Institute for Energy and the Environment.

Study author Mark Cooper, the VLS Institute's senior research fellow for economic analysis, said:

> The problems in the French nuclear industry are similar to the problems that have long afflicted the U.S. industry, so there is no reason to believe that things will change if the U.S. follows the French path.
>
> If the U.S. nuclear industry is relaunched with massive subsidies, this analysis shows the greatest danger is not that the U.S. will import French technology, but that it will replicate the French model of nuclear socialism.
>
> Nuclear power will remain a ward of the state, as has been true throughout its history in France; a great burden on ratepayers, as has been the case throughout its history in both France and the U.S.; and it will retard the development of lower-cost renewables alternatives, as it has done in France and portions of the U.S.

The Cost of Nuclear Power Has Increased Dramatically

Cooper's study [is] titled "Policy Challenges of Nuclear Reactor Construction: Cost Escalation and Crowding Out Alternatives. Lessons from the U.S. and France for the Effort to Revive the U.S. Industry with Loan Guarantees and Tax Subsidies."

Key study findings include the following:

- Nuclear reactors are not cheaper in France. Both the U.S. and French nuclear industries have experienced severe cost escalation in recent years.
- Measured in 2008 dollars, U.S. and French overnight costs were similar in the early 1970s, about $1,000 per kilowatt (kW).

- In the U.S. they escalated to the range of $3,000 to $4,000 per kW by the mid-1980s. The final reactors were generally in the $5,000 to $6,000 range.
- French costs increased to the range of $2,000–$3,000 in the mid-1980s and $3,000 to $5,000 in the 1990s.
- The report finds that the claim that standardization, learning, or large increases in the number (and size) of reactors under construction will lower costs is not supported in the data.
- In France and the U.S. building nuclear reactors and central station facilities crowd out energy efficiency and renewable energy.
- The French track record on energy efficiency and renewables is poor compared to similar European nations. In the U.S., past nuclear construction [and] future nuclear plans appear to crowd out alternatives—a trend that would worsen significantly under large-scale subsidization of nuclear reactors, which mirrors the French model.
- States in which utilities have not expressed an interest in getting licenses for new nuclear reactors have a better track record on efficiency and renewables and more aggressive plans for future development of efficiency and renewables.

States Without Nuclear Power Are More Energy Efficient

With respect to efficiency and renewable energy, the "no nuclear plans" U.S. states have (in comparison to U.S. "nuclear states"): had three times as much renewable energy and ten times as much non-hydro renewable energy in their 1990 generation mix; set Renewable Portfolio Standards (RPS) goals for the next decade that are 50 percent higher; spent three times as much on efficiency in 2006; saved over three times as much energy in the 1992–2006 period; and have much stronger utility efficiency programs in place.

The U.S. would have even more to lose in terms of renewables than France if it followed France's model of more nuclear power.

The World's Nuclear Reactors, 2009

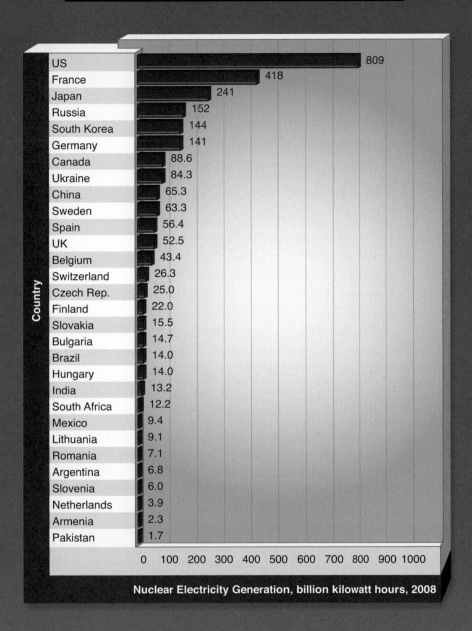

Nuclear Electricity Generation, billion kilowatt hours, 2008

Country	Value
US	809
France	418
Japan	241
Russia	152
South Korea	144
Germany	141
Canada	88.6
Ukraine	84.3
China	65.3
Sweden	63.3
Spain	56.4
UK	52.5
Belgium	43.4
Switzerland	26.3
Czech Rep.	25.0
Finland	22.0
Slovakia	15.5
Bulgaria	14.7
Brazil	14.0
Hungary	14.0
India	13.2
South Africa	12.2
Mexico	9.4
Lithuania	9.1
Romania	7.1
Argentina	6.8
Slovenia	6.0
Netherlands	3.9
Armenia	2.3
Pakistan	1.7

Taken from: *Guardian* (London), "Nuclear Power Around the World," blog entry by Adam Vaughan, November 9, 2009.
www.guardian.co.uk/environment/datablog/2009/aug/14/nuclear-power-world.

According to the new report, the U.S. has a much greater opportunity to develop alternatives not only because the cost disadvantage of nuclear in the U.S. is greater, but also because the portfolio of alternative resources is much greater in the U.S.

The U.S. consumes about 50 percent more electricity per dollar of gross domestic product per capita than France, which has the highest electricity consumption among comparable Western European nations. The U.S. has renewable opportunities that are four times as great as Europe.

The French Nuclear Power Industry Is in Crisis

Commenting on the study, Stephen Thomas, professor of energy studies, University of Greenwich, London, and a member of the editorial boards of Energy Policy, Utility Policy, Energy and Environment, and International Journal of Regulation and Governance, said:

> The French nuclear power industry is in crisis on three counts: its new reactor technology, the Evolutionary Power Reactor (EPR), is proving expensive and difficult to build and gaining safety approval is proving slow and problematic; the existing 58 reactors are far less reliable than its European and US peers; and its flagship nuclear companies, the utility Electricité de France (EDF) and the reactor vendor Areva, are straggling to control their levels of debt.

> This experience suggests that, far from being a model to emulate, the French experience is a cautionary tale of overdependence on nuclear power and on the state becoming too embroiled in commercial decisions.

> Missing from most U.S. discussions of the "French model" is information about the history and recent experience of French nuclear costs, detailed analyses of past U.S. costs and current cost projections and a careful examination of the impact of the decision to promote nuclear reactor and other central station construction on the development of alternative energy sources.

A new Evolutionary Power Reactor (EPR) is constructed in Flammanville, France. Safety approvals have been slow in coming, and the difficult project has proved expensive.

Cooper's paper uses historical qualitative and statistical analysis to fill those gaps.

Cooper explained: "The policy implications of this paper are both narrow and broad. Narrowly, the paper shows that following the French model would be a mistake since the French nuclear reactor program is far less of a success than is assumed, takes an organizational approach that is alien to the U.S. and reflects a very different endowment of energy resources."

He added: "Broadly, the paper shows that it is highly unlikely that the problems of the nuclear industry will be solved by an infusion of federal loan guarantees and other subsidies to get the first plants in a new building cycle completed. U.S. policymakers should resist efforts to force the government into making large loans on terms that put taxpayers at risk in order to 'save' a project or an industry that may not be salvageable."

SIXTEEN

A Teenage Boy Creates a Nuclear Fusion Reactor at Home

Thiago Olsen, as told to Rose Jacobs

> Thiago Olsen, as a seventeen-year-old high school student, built a working nuclear fusion reactor in his garage. In the following viewpoint Olsen describes his device and how he built it. He also explains his idea for making a practical device from the reactor that could be used to detect explosives in sealed containers. As a result of his work, Olsen became part of a small but growing community of self-described "nuclear fusioneers." Rose Jacobs is a reporter for the *Financial Times* in London.

Last month, my high-school principal got a message from the US Department of Health. They wanted to visit my house—or more specifically, to check out a 6x3x2ft. machine I had built in my parents' garage. I call it the Fusor, for obvious reasons: In it, I've created nuclear fusion.

My apparatus doesn't produce more energy than I put in—that's never been done, and if someone can figure it out, they'll be set. But what it does do is create helium by smashing charged hydrogen isotopes together. That's fusion—when two elements fuse together to make a new element, releasing a lot of light and heat in the process.

Thiago Olsen, as told to Rose Jacobs, "There's a Nuke in My Garage: Michigan Teenager Thiago Olsen, 17, Has Taken Schoolboy Science Projects to a New Level," *Financial Times* (London), January 27, 2007, p. 7. Copyright © 2007 Financial Times Information Ltd. Information may not be copied or redistributed. Reproduced by permission.

So two government radiation-safety officers came over to check it out. The fire chief for my area also came over. He came to see the machine—and the fusion—and to make sure there wasn't a fire hazard.

Actually, no one had much to worry about. The biggest danger comes from the high voltage I use to charge a spherical wire grid at the centre of the vacuum chamber (where all the action happens). I charge it up to about negative 40,000 volts, and then inject into the chamber a gas called deuterium—a stable isotope of hydrogen. Because deuterium particles are positively charged, they are attracted to the negative charge at very high velocities—and in the middle, they smash together.

French officials look at an experimental fusion reactor. Thiago Olsen created a similar device in his garage.

The reaction looks like a small star. In a sense, it is a small star, because it's in a vacuum much like space and it's running off the same reaction: E=mc2.

For a long time, I didn't even realise that I was following that equation. When I first started this project, about two years ago, I thought I understood the physics—I had already taken a college-level physics course—but I didn't really understand everything that was going on. Back then, I had been looking for some sort of project to do; I like physics a lot, and science, and I've always been working on science projects, but all the other ones were small compared to this.

Building a Fusion Reactor

When I ran into a website that talked about amateur fusion, I didn't think it was possible—and neither did my father. But after much more research, I decided to go for it. For the first year, I just read about it. And then last year I started buying materials and actually starting to build it.

All of the equipment is really expensive, so I had to get it used or surplus. If there were new parts I really needed, I would e-mail manufacturers telling them my situation and asking if I could have discounts. But most of what I used was old material from government and university labs.

After nearly two years of work and having tested all the components separately in various stages, I didn't want to try running it until I thought it was going to work. So I waited patiently for the UPS truck to show up with the last few pieces of the gas system. And then, on September 20 2006, the first time I actually ran it, I got fusion.

The way you know you have fusion is to look for free neutrons, which rarely, if ever, occur in nature. When the hydrogen particles smash together and join, they release neutrons. A "neutron bubble dosimeter"—a device full of a liquid that only responds to free neutrons—is attached to the Fusor. When I run the reactor, after a few minutes you'll see about 10 bubbles. This equates to roughly 200,000 neutrons per second.

Fusion Reaction

Deuterium (D) and Tritium (T) combine in the fusion reaction to produce a free neutron, Helium (He) and energy.

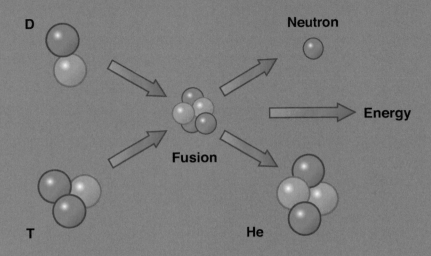

Taken from: *Helian Unbound*, "On Deception Watch—The 'Conspiracy' to Kill Fusion," blog entry by Helian, September 4, 2010. http://helian.net/blog/2010/09/04/inertial-confinement-fusion/on-deception-watch-the-conspiracy-to-kill-fusion. Note: e-mail address is helian@helian.net.

A Practical Application

The neutrons are what have me most interested right now, because they have a practical use. When a neutron hits a certain element, the reaction produces a gamma ray. And every single element has its own signature gamma ray. So you can shoot neutrons at an object, and based on what gamma rays come back, you can identify the object without even seeing it. And neutrons and gamma rays can go through, say, a foot of lead, no problem.

So you could, for example, use neutrons to scan through a suitcase—even a shielded suitcase—or even a whole shipping container. You would get a complete breakdown of every element in the container and you could tell if it had explosives in it because explosives have very high nitrogen content. If you see a big spike in the nitrogen energy level, then you know you've either got a suitcase with explosives or suitcase full of fertilizer—and you shouldn't have either of those at an airport.

That's what I'm hoping to present at a few science competitions coming up this winter. The contests are both around March, which is good, because in the fall and spring, I run cross-country and track. They take up two hours after school, and time on the weekends, and with lots of homework to do as well, I barely have any time to work on the project.

Still, it's going to be a busy winter.

What You Should Know About Nuclear Power

Facts About Nuclear Power

According to the US Department of Energy:

- A typical 1 million kilowatt (1 kilowatt = 1,000 watts) nuclear power plant contains roughly 100 tons of uranium fuel, one-third of which is removed and replaced annually.
- Within ten years the amount of radiation in spent fuel has declined by 90 percent.
- Most nuclear plants are fueled by a specific form of uranium called U-235, because its atoms split apart easily. Although uranium is common, U-235 is relatively rare.
- Uranium fuel is made into ceramic pellets about the size of a human fingertip, each of which makes as much energy as 150 gallons of oil.

The Nuclear Energy Institute reports:

- A 1,000 megawatt (1 megawatt = 1 million watts) reactor operating at 90 percent capacity can produce enough energy in a year [7.9 billion kilowatt-hours] to supply 740,000 households.
- To produce the same amount from oil would require 13.7 million barrels of oil.
- Each year 20 metric tons (1 metric ton = 2,204.6 pounds) of used nuclear fuel is generated by a typical nuclear power plant. The entire nuclear industry creates about 2,300 metric tons of used fuel each year.

- Over the last forty years, the nuclear industry as a whole has produced approximately 62,500 metric tons of spent fuel—enough to cover a football field to a depth of seven yards.
- In nuclear power plants, fuel costs are approximately 28 percent of the total cost of producing electricity, compared to about 80 percent of the cost of electricity production by plants burning coal, natural gas, or oil. As a result, the cost of nuclear-generated electricity is not as dependent on fluctuations in fuel price as electricity produced by fossil-fuel plants.

The International Atomic Energy Agency reports:
- Except where direct access to cheap fossil fuels exists, nuclear power is cost-competitive with other types of electricity generation.
- If nuclear fuel prices doubled, the cost of nuclear-generated electricity would increase by approximately 9 percent, compared to a 31 percent increase for coal [if the cost of coal doubled] and a 66 percent increase for gas-generated power.

Nuclear Power in America
According to the Nuclear Energy Institute:
- There are 104 operating nuclear reactors in the United States.
- Thirty-one states have nuclear reactors.
- In 2009 seven states produced the largest percentage of their electricity from nuclear power: Vermont [72.3 percent], New Jersey [55.1 percent], Connecticut [53.4 percent], South Carolina [52.0 percent], Illinois [48.7 percent], New Hampshire [44.1 percent], and Virginia [39.6 percent].
- The largest nuclear plant in the United States is the Palo Verde plant in Arizona. It has three reactors producing a total of 3,942 MW (megawatts) of electricity.
- The oldest still-operating plant is Oyster Creek in New Jersey, which has been producing electricity since April 1969.
- In 2009, 20.2 percent of US electricity was generated by nuclear power, amounting to 798.7 billion kilowatt-hours.

The US Energy Information Administration reports:
- Illinois has the greatest number of nuclear reactors (eleven) and the largest nuclear capacity.

- The first large-scale commercial nuclear power plant in America opened in 1957 in Shippingport, Pennsylvania.
- The last new commercial reactor completed in the United States is the Watts Bar 1 reactor in Tennessee, which started operating in 1996. Another new reactor, Watts Bar 2, began construction in 2007 and is expected to start operating in 2012.
- As of February 2009, the Nuclear Regulatory Commission had received applications for twenty-six new reactors. It will take almost four years to review those applications and five to seven years to construct each reactor that is approved.
- In 2008 the amount of electricity generated by nuclear power (20 percent) almost equaled the amount produced by natural gas (21 percent).
- The percentage of electricity generated in the United States from nuclear power was 5 percent in 1973, 9 percent in 1975, and 20 percent in 1988.
- As of 2008 the United States had the greatest nuclear capacity of any nation, at 100.3 gigawatts (1 gigawatt = 1 billion watts).

According to the US Department of Energy:
- A nuclear power plant is designed to operate for a minimum of forty years; an operating permit can be extended for an additional twenty years following strict safety reviews.
- Advances in technology have enabled existing nuclear plants to increase electricity generation by 178 billion kilowatt-hours between 1997 and 2007.
- In 2007, 806 billion kilowatt-hours of electricity was produced by the nation's 104 nuclear reactors.
- Building a nuclear plant creates 1,400 to 1,800 temporary construction jobs.
- Over 200 workers are employed at each nuclear power plant for regular operation and maintenance.
- Operating one nuclear power plant creates permanent employment for 400 to 700 people, each making 36 percent more than the average local salary.

As reported in a poll published by the Nuclear Energy Institute in June 2010:

- Seventy-four percent of Americans currently favor nuclear power, compared to 49 percent in 1983.
- Thirty-three percent strongly favor nuclear power, while only 10 percent strongly oppose it.
- Seventy percent of Americans support construction of new nuclear power plants, up from 47 percent in 1998.
- Seventy-seven percent would accept new reactors at existing nuclear power plants.
- Whereas in 1984 only 35 percent of the public felt highly confident of nuclear power plant safety, currently 73 percent express a high degree of confidence. Only 10 percent gave a low safety rating to nuclear plants.
- Only 42 percent of Americans believe the American public supports building more nuclear power plants, whereas 70 percent actually hold that opinion.

The World Nuclear Association reports:

- From 1950 to 2006, all US federal incentives for nuclear power amounted to $65 billion (in 2006 dollars), compared to $93 billion for coal and $436 billion for oil and gas.

Nuclear Power Around the World

According to the Nuclear Energy Institute:

- In 2009, 14 percent of world electricity (2,560 billion kilowatt-hours) was produced by nuclear power.
- As of January 2011, 442 commercial nuclear reactors were producing electricity in 29 countries, and 65 new nuclear power plants were being built in 15 countries.

The World Nuclear Association reports:

- Sixteen countries get at least one-fourth of their electricity from nuclear power. France produces about three-fourths of its electricity from nuclear power, while Belgium, Bulgaria, the Czech Republic, Hungary, Slovakia, South Korea, Sweden, Switzerland, Slovenia, and Ukraine produce one-third or more.

- Germany, Japan, and Finland produce more than one-fourth from nuclear power. The United States produces one-fifth of its electricity via nuclear power.
- Thirty-four percent of the electricity in the European Union is produced by nuclear power.
- From 1990 to 2006, world production of electricity from nuclear power rose by 40 percent (757 billion kilowatt-hours).
- China plans to increase nuclear capacity to 70–80 gigawatts by 2020.
- India plans to build twenty to thirty new nuclear reactors by 2020.
- World production of nuclear-generating capacity will likely be at least 1,130 gigawatts by 2060 [compared to 373 gigawatts at present], and could be as high as 3,500 gigawatts.
- Currently the world makes as much electricity from nuclear power as the total amount produced by all sources in 1960.
- In 1999 world production of uranium totaled 31,065 metric tons, compared to a total production of 50,772 metric tons in 2009.
- In addition to commercial reactors, 56 countries have about 250 operating research reactors; there are, as well, 140 ships and submarines powered by 180 reactors.
- In total, civilian nuclear power has over 14,000 years of cumulative reactor-years' experience.

According to the International Atomic Energy Agency:
- By 2030 projections indicate an increase in nuclear generating capacity worldwide of at least 35 percent, and possibly as high as 120 percent.
- The year 2008 was the only year since 1955 that did not see a single new reactor start operations; however, construction was begun on ten new reactors that year—the most since 1987.
- In 2009, two new nuclear reactors came online, and construction was begun on an additional twelve nuclear reactors.
- The number of new reactors being built rose from 33 with a combined capacity of 27,193 megawatts in 2007 to 60 with a combined capacity of 58,584 megawatts as of August 26, 2010.

- The average reactor size operating in 2010 was 850 megawatts.
- An estimated 250,000 people were employed in nuclear power plants around the world in 2009.
- Uranium mining is being undertaken in nineteen countries, with eight supplying 93 percent of total world capacity.
- Sixty-five countries have expressed interest in, are considering, or are planning to pursue nuclear power. Twenty-one are in Asia and the Pacific region, twenty-one are in Africa, twelve in Europe, and eleven in Latin America.
- Twenty-five countries planning their first nuclear plant have target dates before 2030, including fourteen that plan to start operations by 2020.
- Of those countries planning for nuclear power, twenty-four have at least one research reactor.
- In 2009, 76.23 percent of electricity in Lithuania was produced by nuclear power; France produced 75.17 percent; and the United States produced 20.17 percent.

Nuclear Power and Climate Change

According to the US Department of Energy:
- Nuclear power is the largest source of electricity that does not release significant amounts of greenhouse gases, supplying about 20 percent of America's electricity. Hydroelectric power, the second-largest nonemitting source, supplies about 7 percent. Wind and solar power each supply about 2 percent.
- Nuclear power supplies about 70 percent of the non-greenhouse gas-emitting electricity produced in America.
- Each megawatt hour of electricity produced by nuclear power prevents the release of about 1 million metric tons of carbon dioxide that would have been created by using coal-fired technologies to generate that power, or 0.6 million metric tons that would be produced by using natural gas.

The Nuclear Energy Institute reports:
- Nuclear power stations generate 45 percent of carbon-free electricity in the world.

- Each year nuclear power around the world prevents the release of 2.6 billion metric tons of carbon dioxide.
- In the United States, electricity generated by nuclear plants prevents the emission of about 650 million metric tons of carbon dioxide each year, which is almost as much as is released by all US cars.

The International Atomic Energy Agency, in a 2009 report titled *Climate Change and Nuclear Power*, states:

- Without strong policy intervention, CO_2 (carbon dioxide, the main greenhouse gas) emissions will increase 55 percent by 2030 and 130 percent by 2050. However, in order to prevent unacceptable levels of climate change, emissions would need to be reduced by 50 to 80 percent by 2050.
- In 2007 global CO_2 emissions from generation of electricity was 11.1 billion metric tons, but would have been 13.4 billion metric tons in the absence of nuclear power generation.

What You Should Do About Nuclear Power

Gather Information

The first step in grappling with any complex and controversial issue is to be informed about it. Gather as much information as you can from a variety of sources. The essays in this book form an excellent starting point, representing a variety of viewpoints and approaches to the topic. Your school or local library will be another source of useful information; look there for relevant books, magazines, and encyclopedia entries. The bibliography and "Organizations to Contact" sections of this book will give you useful starting points in gathering additional information.

Internet search engines will be helpful to you in your search. Many blogs and websites have information and articles dealing with nuclear power from a variety of perspectives, including concerned individuals offering their opinions, advocacy and activist organizations, popular media outlets, and governmental and scientific organizations.

Identify the Issues Involved

Once you have gathered your information, review it methodically to discover the key issues involved. How does nuclear power compare to other sources of power such as fossil fuels, solar power, etc., both in terms of environmental impact and ability to supply the world's energy needs? Does nuclear power have an impact on nuclear weapons proliferation or potential terrorist attacks? What safeguards are in place to deal with those issues? How big a problem is nuclear waste, and how is that problem being addressed? How does the threat of climate change affect the debate over nuclear power? What has been the impact of nuclear accidents such as those at Three Mile Island and Chernobyl, and what has been learned from such incidents?

Notice how much disagreement there is on many basic aspects of nuclear power. The Chernobyl accident that took place in 1986 in the former Soviet Union is a particularly useful example. Many articles and books have been written on the subject in the decades since the disaster that come to very different conclusions. Arguments are made that the expected death toll from the radioactive contamination has been much greater than the official figures, while others claim there has been a much lower than expected health impact—and both sides cite convincing studies to support their arguments.

In grappling with this issue it may also be useful to look at how attitudes toward nuclear power have changed over time, as well as how the issues are thought about and dealt with by various cultures around the world.

Evaluate Your Information Sources

In developing your own opinion, it is vital to evaluate the sources of the information you have discovered. Authors of books, magazine articles, and so forth, however well intentioned, have their own perspectives and biases that may affect how they present information on the subject. This is particularly true of a highly charged issue like nuclear power.

Consider the authors' credentials and organizational affiliations. They may offer information that is perfectly valid, but will emphasize data that support their viewpoint and that of the organization they are associated with. In some cases they may even distort or ignore information in order to make their case. An environmental organization staunchly opposed to nuclear power, for example, may emphasize frightening statistics on how long some radioactive materials take to fully break down. A pro-nuclear organization or industry spokesperson might stress how quickly most of the radioactivity dissipates, or talk about procedures to safeguard nuclear waste.

On the other hand, if you find someone arguing against his or her expected bias—for example, someone who works for the nuclear industry warning of inadequate safety procedures, or an environmentalist who long opposed nuclear power now speaking in favor of it—you may find it worthwhile to pay particular attention to what they are saying. Always critically evaluate and assess your sources rather than take whatever they say at face value.

Examine Your Own Perspective

Consider your own beliefs, feelings, and biases on this subject. Perhaps you have been influenced by the attitudes of family or friends or by media reports. Nuclear power tends to be a highly charged issue for many people and has often been portrayed in extreme and frightening ways in news reports and popular books and movies. If you had a position on nuclear power before reading this book, consider what it might take to change your mind. Seek out and consider information and perspectives that differ from what you already believe to be true. Be aware of the tendency to look for evidence that confirms what you already believe to be true and to discount anything that contradicts your viewpoint.

You may want to consider how nuclear power might be regarded if it was invented for the first time today, or if the first nuclear reactors had been developed to produce power during a time of peace, rather than being used to make material for the atomic bombs dropped on Japan at the end of World War II. Thought experiments such as these can help you to approach a controversial issue with a fresh perspective and a beginner's mind.

Form Your Own Opinion and Take Action

Once you have gathered and organized information, identified the issues involved, and examined your own perspective, you will be ready to form an opinion on nuclear power and to advocate that position in debates and discussions. Perhaps you will come to the conclusion that nuclear power is too dangerous to use and should be phased out as quickly as possible. You may conclude that the risks of nuclear power have been vastly overstated or that the nuclear industry has learned how to deal with real or potential problems in a responsible manner. Or you may find yourself in agreement with those who believe that while there is some danger in using nuclear power, the risk of climate change from other forms of energy is far greater and that nuclear power is a necessary part of the solution to that planetary crisis. Regardless of the conclusion you draw, you can find people and organizations with similar perspectives who are striving to make changes in the world in accordance with those beliefs.

The editors have compiled the following list of organizations concerned with the issues debated in this book. The descriptions are derived from materials provided by the organizations. All have publications or information available for interested readers. The list was compiled on the date of publication of the present volume; the information provided here may change. Be aware that many organizations take several weeks or longer to respond to inquiries, so allow as much time as possible for the receipt of requested materials.

American Nuclear Society
555 N. Kensington Ave., La Grange Park, IL 60526
(800) 323-3044 • website: www.new.ans.org

The American Nuclear Society was established in 1954 to promote the understanding of nuclear science and technology. The organization is made up of eleven thousand scientists, educators, and other professionals who are committed to unifying those working in nuclear technologies. The American Nuclear Society publishes the journals *Nuclear Science and Engineering*, *Nuclear News*, *Fusion Science and Technology*, and *Radwaste Solutions*.

Canadian Nuclear Safety Commission (CNSC)
280 Slater St. • PO Box 1046, Station B, Ottawa, ON, K1P 5S9
(800) 668-5284 or (613) 995-5894 • e-mail: info@cnsc-ccsn.gc.ca
website: www.cnsc-ccsn.gc.ca/eng

The CNSC was established in 2000 and is tasked with protecting the health, safety, and security of Canadians, as well as the environment, and supporting Canada's international commitments on the peaceful use of nuclear energy. Its website offers a variety of information on the nuclear industry in Canada.

Energy Information Association (EIA)
1000 Independence Ave. SW, Washington, DC 20585
(202) 586-8800 • e-mail: infoctr@eia.doe.gov
website: www.eia.doe.gov

The EIA provides data and analysis to assist in energy policy making. The association also seeks to increase public understanding of energy production, including nuclear power. It collects data and analyzes energy markets, trading, and supply and demand as well as importing and exporting of energy sources. The EIA is divided into four programs that study various energy-related topics.

Green America (GA)
1612 K St. NW, Ste. 600, Washington, DC 20006
(800) 584-7336 • website: www.coopamerica.org

The GA (formerly known as Co-Op America) was founded in 1982. The organization is opposed to the use of nuclear power and takes issue with it as a means to attack global warming. Its website includes a list of ten reasons why nuclear power is not the answer to global energy and environmental concerns. These reasons include nuclear waste toxicity, danger of nuclear proliferation, threat to national security, risk of accidents, risk of cancer from radiation, and others. The GA produces several publications, including *National Green Pages*, *Real Green*, *Green American*, and *Guide to Socially Responsible Investing*.

Greenpeace
702 H St. NW, Ste. 300, Washington, DC 20001
(800) 722-6995 • e-mail: info@wdc.greenpeace.org
website: www.greenpeace.org

Greenpeace was formed in 1971 when a small group of activists chartered a fishing boat and set off to protest nuclear testing off the coast of Alaska. The organization continues to stage peaceful protests against the use of nuclear power while standing up for renewable energy sources. The organization contends that nuclear power is a dangerous distraction from true solutions to increasing demand for energy and worsening global warming. Greenpeace seeks to educate policy makers and the international public by publishing annual reports and fact sheets on global warming and nuclear energy.

International Atomic Energy Agency (IAEA)

1 United Nations Plaza, Rm. DC-1-1155, New York, NY 10017
(212) 963-6010 or 6011 • e-mail: iaeany@un.org
website: www.iaea.or.at

The IAEA was established in 1957 with help from the United Nations as an international Atoms for Peace organization. The agency works with its members to promote the safe and peaceful use of nuclear technologies. The IAEA has offices in Vienna, Austria; Geneva, Switzerland; Toronto, Canada; Tokyo, Japan; and New York. It employs more than twenty-two hundred staff members in ninety countries to ensure that nuclear power and technology policy making include safety and security, safeguards and verification, and the promotion of nuclear science. The agency makes annual reports to the UN General Assembly and Security Council on matters of international peace and safety. The IAEA publishes several scientific journals and papers, including *Effective Nuclear Regulatory Systems: Facing Safety and Security Challenges* and *Innovative and Adaptive Technologies in Decommissioning of Nuclear Facilities*, as well as the *IAEA Bulletin*.

Nuclear Energy Institute (NEI)

1776 I St. NW, Ste. 400, Washington, DC 20006-3708
(202) 739-8000 • e-mail: media@nei.org
website: www.nei.org

The NEI is the policy organization for the nuclear energy and technology industry. The institute works both within the United States and globally to form policies that further the use of nuclear technology and energy around the world. Members include more than three hundred corporations in fifteen countries that work together to promote the safe use of nuclear power to generate electricity as well as the relicensing of nuclear power plants currently in operation. The NEI publishes *Nuclear Energy Insight*, *Nuclear Policy Outlook*, *Perspective on Public Opinion*, and *Nuclear Performance Monthly*.

Nuclear Information and Resource Service (NIRS)
6390 Carroll Ave., Ste. 340, Takoma Park, MD 20912
(301) 270-6477 • e-mail: nirsnet@nirs.org
website: www.nirs.org/home.htm

The NIRS was formed in the 1970s to educate the public on the dangers of nuclear energy and technology. It has expanded to become a global watchdog group that adamantly opposes the construction of new nuclear power plants. The NIRS organizes protests and campaigns against using nuclear energy. It also seeks to change global energy policies to focus on renewable sources such as wind and solar power.

Office of Nuclear Energy
1000 Independence Ave. SW, Washington, DC 20585
(800) 342-5363 • e-mail: the.secretary@hq.doe.gov
website: www.ne.doe.gov

The Office of Nuclear Energy is a department within the US Department of Energy that focuses on promoting nuclear power in the United States. Its mission is to encourage the Department of Energy to invest in the development of nuclear science and technology and to develop new nuclear energy technologies. It also seeks to develop proliferation-resistant nuclear fuel and to maintain national nuclear facilities. In addition to a wealth of information on nuclear energy, the website has a special section for students available from the main page or at www.ne.doe.gov/students/intro.html.

Open Source Fusor Research Consortium
c/o Cohesion Arts, Box 210294, Nashville, TN 37221
e-mail: blog@49chevy.com • website: www.fusor.net

The Open Source Fusor Research Consortium is a website catering to the "fusioneer" community of amateurs (including some high school students), who build low-power nuclear fusion reactors in their basements and garages. The website contains detailed instructions on how to construct this type of fusion reactor, as well as links to relevant websites and a lively discussion forum.

Radiation Information Network (RIN)
Department of Health Physics
Idaho State University, Campus Box 8106, Pocatello, ID 83209
(208) 282-2350 • e-mail: office@physics.isu.edu
website: www.physics.isu.edu/radinf

The RIN is run by professors and students within the Department of Health Physics at Idaho State University. It collects the latest research and information about radiation for those who work in the radiation protection industry as well as for anyone interested in learning more about its effects. The RIN seeks to educate the public about regulatory and professional information regarding radiation.

World Nuclear Association (WNA)
22a Saint Jame's Square, London, SW1Y 4JH United Kingdom
+44 20 7451 1520 • e-mail: wna@world-nuclear.org
website: www.world-nuclear.org

The WNA is a private international organization committed to the peaceful use of nuclear power. It believes that nuclear power is a sustainable solution to global energy needs and is interested in furthering nuclear technologies and education. The WNA publishes papers on nuclear fuel production, industry economics, trade issues, radiological safety, transporting nuclear materials, decommissioning nuclear power plants, handling radioactive waste, sustainability of nuclear energy, security, and safety. The association also publishes the brochure *Four Pillars of Support for a Fast-Globalizing Nuclear Industry*.

World Wildlife Fund (WWF)
1250 Twenty-Fourth St. NW, Washington, DC 20585
(202) 495-4800 • website: www.panda.org

The WWF was created in 1961 by a few concerned world citizens and has since grown into one of the world's largest environmental organizations. The organization has more than thirteen hundred conservation projects around the world. It is seriously concerned with the threat nuclear energy and technology pose to humans, animals, and the environment. The WWF is adamantly opposed to nuclear power, believing it poses serious security risks and will distract from creating innovative clean energy alternatives. The following downloadable publications are available on its website: *WWF Position Statement on Nuclear Power, Why Not Nuclear Power?, Climate Change and Nuclear Power*, and *Climate Solutions: WWF's Vision for 2050*.

Yucca Mountain Information Office

PO Box 990, Eureka, NV 89316
(775) 237-5707 • e-mail: ecyucca@eurekanv.org
website: www.yuccamountain.org

The Eureka County, Nevada, government started this organization to keep its residents apprised of the history and current developments regarding the Yucca Mountain Depository project. Residents of Eureka and other interested parties can follow the progress of this proposed—and controversial—permanent nuclear waste dump with information provided by the Yucca Mountain Information Office. Tools offered to the public include a time line, maps, litigation information, and a quarterly newsletter.

BIBLIOGRAPHY

Books

Stewart Brand, *Whole Earth Discipline: An Ecopragmatist Manifesto*. New York: Viking, 2009.

Helen Caldicott, *Nuclear Power Is Not the Answer*. New York: New Press, 2006.

Gwyneth Cravens, *Power to Save the World: The Truth About Nuclear Energy*. New York: Knopf, 2007.

Alan M. Herbst and George W. Hopley, *Nuclear Energy Now: Why the Time Has Come for the World's Most Misunderstood Energy Source*. Hoboken, NJ: Wiley, 2007.

Ian Hore-Lacy, *Nuclear Energy in the 21st Century*. London: World Nuclear University Press, 2006.

Igor Kostine and Johnson Thomas, *Chernobyl: Confessions of a Reporter*. New York: Umbrage, 2006.

Ian Lowe and Barry Brook, *WHY vs. WHY Nuclear Power* Sydney. Australia: Pantera, 2010.

John Meany, *Is Nuclear Power Safe?* Chicago: Heinemann Library, 2008.

R. Muller, *Physics for Future Presidents: The Science Behind the Headlines*. New York: Norton, 2008.

Joseph M. Shuster, *Beyond Fossil Fools: The Roadmap to Energy Independence by 2040*. Edina, MN: Beaver's Pond, 2008.

Ken Silverstein, *The Radioactive Boy Scout: The Frightening True Story of a Whiz Kid and His Homemade Nuclear Reactor*. New York: Villard, 2005.

Neal Singer, *Wonders of Nuclear Fusion: Creating an Ultimate Energy Source*. Albuquerque: University of New Mexico Press, 2011.

Brice Smith, *Insurmountable Risks: The Dangers of Using Nuclear Power to Combat Global Climate Change*. Takoma Park, MD: IEER, 2006.

John Townsend, *Using Nuclear Energy*. Chicago: Heinemann Library, 2009.

William Tucker, *Terrestrial Energy: How Nuclear Power Will Lead the Green Revolution and End America's Energy Odyssey*. Savage, MD: Bartleby, 2008.

Tom Zoellner, *Uranium: War, Energy, and the Rock That Shaped the World*. New York: Viking: 2009.

Periodicals and Internet Sources

Thomas Backus, "What to Do with Nuclear Waste? The Rise and Fall of Yucca Mountain," *Student Pulse Academic Journal*, March 23, 2010. www.studentpulse.com/articles/212/what-to-do-with-nuclear-waste-the-rise-and-fall-of-yucca-mountain.

David Biello, "Finding Fissile Fuel," *Scientific American*, January 26, 2009. www.scientificamerican.com/article.cfm?id=finding-fissile-fuel.

Peter Bradford, "Honey, I Shrunk the Renaissance: Nuclear Revival, Climate Change, and Reality," *Clean Energy*, October 15, 2010. http://blog.cleanenergy.org/2010/10/15/failed-nuclear-revival/.

Stewart Brand, "Why Environmentalists Must Accept Nuclear," *Big Think*, December 11, 2009. http://bigthink.com/ideas/17724.

Helen Caldicott and Dale Dewar, "Nuclear Radiation Is Forever," *Common Dreams*, February 8, 2011. www.commondreams.org/view/2011/02/08-6.

Gwyneth Cravens, "Is Nuclear Energy Our Best Hope?," *Discover*, April 24, 2008. http://discovermagazine.com/2008/may/02-is-nuclear-energy-our-best-hope.

Matthew Danzico, "Extreme DIY: Building a Homemade Nuclear Reactor in NYC," BBC, June 23, 2010. www.bbc.co.uk/news/10385853.

Paul Davidson, "Nuclear Power Inches Back into Energy Spotlight," *USA Today*, March 30, 2009. www.usatoday.com/money/industries/energy/environment/2009-03-29-nuclear-power-energy-return_N.htm.

Peter Hessler, "The Uranium Widows," *New Yorker*, September 13, 2010.

Mara Hvistendahl, "Coal Ash Is More Radioactive than Nuclear Waste," *Scientific American*, December 13, 2007. www.sciam .com/article.cfm?id=coal-ash-is-more-radioactive-than-nuclear-waste.

Xeni Jardin, "How Tough Is It to Build a Dirty Bomb?," *Boing Boing*, February 9, 2011. www.boingboing.net/2011/02/09/how-tough-is-it-to-b.html.

Daniel Kessler, "'Clean' Nuclear Power? The President Knows Better," *Huffington Post*, January 28, 2010. www.huffingtonpost .com/daniel-kessler/clean-nuclear-power-the-p_b_440710.html.

Maggie Koerth-Baker, "The Blue Flash: Nuclear Accidents and the Origins of Superhero Origins," *Boing Boing*, February 8, 2011. www.boingboing.net/2009/10/30/the-blue-flash-nucle.html.

Juliet Lapidos, "Atomic Priesthoods, Thorn Landscapes, and Munchian Pictograms: How to Communicate the Dangers of Nuclear Waste to Future Civilizations," *Slate*, November 16, 2009. www.slate.com/id/2235504.

Ilya Leybovich, "Is Nuclear Fusion Too Sci-Fi to Work?," *ThomasNet News*, July 20, 2010. http://news.thomasnet.com/ imt/archives/2010/07/is-nuclear-fusion-too-sci-fi-to-work.html.

Amory Lovins, "Forget Nuclear," *Rocky Mountain Institute*, 2008. www.rmi.org/rmi/Library/E08-04_ForgetNuclear.

Alexis Madrigal, "Chernobyl Exclusion Zone Radioactive Longer than Expected," *Wired*, December 15, 2009. www.wired.com/ wiredscience/2009/12/chernobyl-soil.

Rob Margetta, "Maritime Cargo Scanning: The Wrong Approach for Avoiding Nuclear Attack?," *CQ Homeland Security*, August 19, 2010.

Lauren Monaghan, "Silent Spring," *Cosmos*, June 2008. www .cosmosmagazine.com/node/2095/full.

Margot Roosevelt, "Nuclear Waste: The Swedish Example," *Los Angeles Times*, February 20, 2010. http://latimesblogs.latimes

.com/greenspace/2010/02/nuclear-waste-yucca-mountain-sweden.html.

Lawrence Solomon, "Radiation's Benefits," *Financial Post*, September 24, 2010. http://opinion.financialpost.com/2010/09/24/lawrence-solomon-radiations-benefits.

Claire Thomas, "Cleaning Up Depleted Uranium with Fungi," *Cosmos*, May 14, 2008. www.cosmosmagazine.com/news/1987/cleaning-depleted-uranium-with-fungi.

Michael Totty, "Nuclear's Fall—and Rise," *Wall Street Journal*, April 17, 2010. http://online.wsj.com/article/SB10001424052702303411604575168171976855444.html.

Harvey Wasserman, "Stewart Brand Is Wrong About Nukes—and Is Losing," *Huffington Post*, July 26, 2010. www.huffingtonpost.com/harvey-wasserman/stewart-brand-is-wrong-ab_b_658796.html.

Melanie S. Welte, "Nuclear Power Fought with Social Media by New Generation of Activists," *Huffington Post*, August 28, 2010. www.huffingtonpost.com/2010/08/30/nuclear-power-fought-with_n_698833.html.

Christine Todd Whitman, "The Case for Nuclear Power Is as Strong as Ever," *Huffington Post*, August 2, 2010. www.huffingtonpost.com/christine-todd-whitman/the-case-for-nuclear-powe_b_667193.html.

World Nuclear Association, "Chernobyl Accident," February 2011. www.world-nuclear.org/info/chernobyl/inf07.html.

World Nuclear Association, "Three Mile Island Accident," January 2010. www.world-nuclear.org/info/inf36.html.

Lisa Zyga, "Mini Nuclear Power Plants Could Power 20,000 Homes," *Physorg*, November 12, 2008. www.physorg.com/news145561984.html.

INDEX

PICTURE CREDITS